Walter Lowrie

The Doctrine of Saint John

An Essay in Biblical Theology

Walter Lowrie

The Doctrine of Saint John
An Essay in Biblical Theology

ISBN/EAN: 9783337336615

Printed in Europe, USA, Canada, Australia, Japan

Cover: Foto ©Lupo / pixelio.de

More available books at **www.hansebooks.com**

THE DOCTRINE OF SAINT JOHN

An Essay in Biblical Theology

BY

WALTER LOWRIE, M.A.

MISSION PRIEST IN THE CITY MISSION, PHILADELPHIA

LONGMANS, GREEN, AND CO.
91 AND 93 FIFTH AVENUE, NEW YORK
LONDON AND BOMBAY
1899

Copyright, 1899,
BY LONGMANS, GREEN, AND CO.

All rights reserved.

University Press:
JOHN WILSON AND SON, CAMBRIDGE, U.S.A.

TO THE

VERY LEARNED FACULTY
OF
Princeton Theological Seminary,
TO WHOSE TUITION I OWE THE INCEPTION OF THIS STUDY,
AS I OWE ITS COMPLETION TO THE OPPORTUNITY
OF FOREIGN STUDY WHICH I ENJOYED AS
NON-RESIDENT FELLOW OF
THEIR SCHOOL,

I HAVE THE HONOR TO DEDICATE
THIS BOOK.

N. B. — The system of scripture reference which is here adopted has for some years been used in Germany, and has been lately adopted in certain standard English works. It is especially convenient for the present purpose, since the references are in the main to but two books, the Gospel and the First Epistle of S. John. The larger numeral refers to the chapter; the smaller, to the verse. The Gospel is always intended when no other reference is indicated, expressly or in the context. S. John's Epistles are denoted by the Roman numerals I., II., and III. Other writings are quoted by name, abbreviated as usual.

Preface

THIS essay was originally presented as an academic thesis. During the years which have since elapsed, I have followed up the study with interest, although I have never had time to devote myself professedly to it. This presentation of the subject, although it is far more than a mere revision, reproduces substantially the conception of the earlier study; and it is set forth with the more confidence, because it has thus stood the test of time, of broader study, and of more mature reflection.

This essay aims at interpreting the theology of S. John as a whole. There is an abundance of detailed exegetical studies of S. John's writings; there are also many valuable studies of the several component parts of S. John's theology: but it appears as if no one had seriously undertaken to do for S. John what has in a measure been accomplished in the case of S. Paul; — to give such an exposition of his thought as shall comprise, not only all of his theology — in the sense that every topic of his theology is discussed between the covers of a single book, — but his theology as a whole, as a system. It would not be difficult to arrange the several topics of the Johannine doctrine according to the familiar rubrics of ecclesiastical theology or according to any arbitrary scheme; but it is a matter of very great difficulty, as it is also of very great importance, to arrange S. John's doctrine according to a system which reflects the peculiar complexion of his own thought. It is chiefly in this respect that this essay may claim to be an independent contribution. To this interest, to the aim of giving a total impression of S. John's theology as an organic unity, every thing has been subordinated, and something perhaps sacrificed in the discussion of the several parts. A glance at the table of contents will show with how much care the construction of S. John's doctrinal system has been studied. I cannot claim that this scheme is established beyond the need of revision; the only hope one can cherish in such a case is that it may approve itself to be a more or less close approximation to the normal, natural development of S. John's doctrine. It will attest its own correctness just in so far as it avails to illuminate S. John's specific doctrines, and to render intelligible their correlation.

I had hoped that, by dwelling upon the salient features of S. John's doctrine, by making prominent the unity of his thought, by omitting technical details, literary references, and any thing which might interfere with the smooth continuity of the exposition, this book might be made available for a far larger circle of readers than is accustomed to interest itself in theological science. That purpose I have had in mind throughout; and although, in reviewing the work, I cannot claim that I have altogether succeeded, I still cannot devise any way to make it easier reading without making it the poorer. The subject is in itself peculiarly fit to enlist a popular interest; in importance it is not inferior to any theme which can occupy the human mind; and with the attention which it undeniably deserves it will be found at least as easy of comprehension as the system of any pagan philosopher.

I have made in the text almost no references to authorities, but I cannot forbear mentioning here a few books which have proved of capital importance for this study. If I mention first the well known work of Bernard Weiss, " Der johanneische Lehrbegriff," it is less as an expression of satisfaction with its treatment, than as an acknowledgment of the fact that it has had a leading influence in the study of the subject, and remains to-day the only book — with the exception of the recent work of Professor Stevens of Yale University — which deals exclusively with the Johannine theology, and professes to give a complete representation of it. There are other works to which I must acknowledge more serious obligation, although they are but indirect or partial contributions to the study: E. Haupt, " Com. on the 1st Epistle of John," Eng. trans.; Franke, "Das Alte Testament bei Johannes;" Schlatter, " Der Glaube im Neuen Testament." It will be readily recognised that a work like the present must be far more broadly indebted than this scant acknowledgment would reveal.

Biblical theology draws its material from so many sources that it would be impossible to remember, even were it thought worth while to note, where credit ought to be bestowed. But no fellow augur will see in the smoothness of the text an evidence of scant labour; nor, it is to be hoped, will the unlearned see therein an undue claim to originality.

This essay was not designed in the interest of apology: nothing in fact could be further from the spirit in which the study was begun. But it is evident that the study of the Johannine writings cannot be pursued without eventually facing and settling the question of their genuineness and authenticity. Biblical theology cannot be altogether divorced from such problems, and they are consequently discussed in the introduction, though only so far as is necessary for the understanding of S. John's thought.

I trust that the avowal that this book is a work of imagination will not raise a prejudice against it as though it were therefore bereft of any solid foundation in fact. Nowhere within the sphere of biblical study is the faculty of imagination so indispensable as in this work of literary interpretation. It is in precisely the same sense, and without the least prejudice to reality, that imagination is a requisite of all higher scientific work; and in the case of historical, as well as in that of physical science, the only applicable test of truth is this: whether the imaginative construction — the hypothesis — is able to account for the facts. One might set to work to interpret the Johannine writings upon the hypothesis that the author was an Alexandrian under the influence of Philo's philosophy, or an antagonist of the gnosticism of the second century, or himself a gnostic, or a Gentile Christian of the second generation under the influence of S. Paul. Some constructive hypothesis one must have, all of these have been maintained, and I treasure the hope that the working hypothesis of the present essay: namely, that the author was a Galilean, a companion of the Lord, and no other than the Apostle John who according to unimpeachable tradition survived all other apostles and proclaimed the message in an age when he alone could say "I saw;" — that this hypothesis may prove itself adequate as no other can to the test of illuminating the characteristics of the Johannine writings, and in so far dispose of the prejudice against their authenticity, which, despite the remarkable accessions of external evidence and the significant admissions on the score of internal criticism, intrenches itself in the assertion that the doctrinal system of the Johannine writings is such as could not have been formulated by the Galilean companion of Jesus — a proposition which in the last resort is founded upon the conviction that one who had personally known Jesus as *a man* could not believe Him to be *God*.

WALTER LOWRIE.

PHILADELPHIA, June, 1899.

CONTENTS

INTRODUCTION

BIBLICAL THEOLOGY IN GENERAL — 3-9

Common recognition of the importance of Biblical Theology.

Vagueness of the prevalent conceptions of it.

Definition of Biblical Theology.

> It is not a rectification of Systematic Theology;
> nor a study of detached ideas;
> nor a mere topical arrangement of the results of exegesis.
>
> It is the exposition of the author's thought *as a whole* according to the relation of emphasis, of co-ordination and sub-ordination, which the different terms had for him.
>
> It is an *historical* study; — an interpretation of the author in terms of his own philosophic method; not a translation into equivalent modes of modern thought.

Method of study.

> Sources: the genuine writings, — and documents which reveal phases of contemporary thought with which the author was in touch.
>
> Helps: commentaries, and special studies of the characteristics and the doctrinal ideas of the New Testament.
>
> Comparative construction: the characteristic labour of Biblical Theology.

Method of exposition.

INTRODUCTION — *continued*

SPECIAL PROBLEMS INVOLVED IN THE STUDY
OF THE DOCTRINE OF S. JOHN 10–17

    Problems peculiar to the study of each author.
        Depending upon the extent and character of the literary sources;
        and upon the date and possible affinities of the author.

    Various claims in respect to the date and affinities of the Johannine writings must be examined.

    Peculiar character of the Johannine sources and their value for Biblical Theology.

        Genuineness of the Gospel and the Epistles, — and the Revelation.

        A normal expression of the author's thought without controversial bias.

        Valuation of the Gospel as a source of Johannine theology :
            the speeches of Jesus, — assimilation of Jesus' teaching in S. John's own thought.
            character and arrangement of the composition an index of the author's point of view.

THE DOCTRINE OF S. JOHN

GENERAL CHARACTERISTICS OF S. JOHN'S THOUGHT 21-46

> The leading peculiarities of the Johannine writings are an index to the fundamental characteristics of the author's thought.
>
> The comparison with the Synoptic Gospels reveals the distinct aim of S. John's work.
>> The author's acquaintance with the Synoptists.
>>
>> Correction, explanation, and supplement of the tradition can be regarded as aims only in a very subsidiary degree.
>>
>> The distinguishing mark of the Fourth Gospel is the character of its representation of the significance of the Person of Christ.
>>
>> The pre-eminent aim of the author is seen to be a teaching which relative to Christ's Person was higher;—not than the belief current in the Church, but than the representation of any previous account of the Lord's life.
>>
>> This fundamental difference between the Synoptists and the Fourth Gospel is explained by the fact that the latter *alone* was written by a companion of the Lord.
>>
>> The combination of a preponderating representation of the subjective significance of Christ's manifestation with the most emphatic contention for its objective reality, is explained by the historical position of the author.
>
> The intuitional character of S. John's thought, in contrast to a speculative or dialectical method.
>
> The constant and close attachment of S. John's thought to the Person of Christ as the revelation of the Father.
>
> The Aramaic traits of S. John's language furnish a hint of the Hebraic affinities of his thought.
>
> Construction of the Johannine theology.

SCHEME OF ARRANGEMENT OF S. JOHN'S DOCTRINE

I. GOD 49–72

GOD IS LIGHT 49–57

    God the centre of theology.
    The meaning of "Light."

THE TRUE GOD 57–63
        ὁ ἀληθινός; אמת.

THE FATHER 63–72

    (The personality of God.)
    (God the Creator.)

Fatherhood in a real sense.— ὁ γεννήσας.
    The only begotten Son.
    The children of God.
    God the source of life.

Fatherhood in an ethical sense.
    The Father and the Nation.
    The Father and the Son.
    The Father and the children.
    God is love.

SCHEME OF ARRANGEMENT OF S. JOHN'S DOCTRINE — *continued*

II. THE LOGOS WITH GOD 73–94

JESUS' SELF-WITNESS 73–82

The only begotten Son.
Divinity of the Son.
Pre-existence of the Son.

S. JOHN'S DOCTRINE OF THE LOGOS 82–94

S. John's own estimate of Christ.
S. John's use of the term Logos.
The motive of S. John's choice of the term.
Content of S. John's doctrine of the Logos.

III. THE KOSMOS LYING IN DARKNESS 95–112

THE WORLD AS THE SPHERE OF HUMAN LIFE 95–98

S. John's slight interest in the material aspects of the world.
Heaven and earth.
The material chaos is the analogy of the ethical darkness.

THE DARKNESS 98–112

The revelation of the old covenant.
The Jews in the Fourth Gospel.
Sin.

IV. THE LIFE MANIFESTED 113-216

THE PARALLEL WITH THE FIRST CHAPTERS OF GENESIS 113-118

THE WORD BECOME FLESH 118-127

The nature of the Incarnation.
The Son of man.
The Messiah.
The Incarnation a manifestation of God's glory.

A. SALVATION OUT OF THE WORLD 128-155

1. THE WHOLE WORLD AS THE OBJECT OF SALVATION.
2. THE DIVISION AMONGST MEN.
3. THE DOOM OF THE WORLD.
4. THE ELECTION OF THE CHILDREN OF GOD OUT OF THE WORLD.

   God's election.
   The covenant people.
   The sacrifice and lustration of the Covenant.

B. REALISATION OF THE POSITIVE CONCEPT OF SALVATION THROUGH THE REVELATION OF THE TRUTH, (or THE APPROPRIATION OF LIFE) . . . 156-216

THE NEW BIRTH. — THE LIGHT OF LIFE 162-186
   Christ the Truth.
   The Spirit of truth.
   Believing and knowing.

ETERNAL LIFE 186-194

THE CHILDREN OF GOD. — FELLOWSHIP 194-216
   Theology and ethics.
   Likeness to God.
   The new commandment.
   Confidence.
   Prayer.

INTRODUCTION

INTRODUCTION

BIBLICAL THEOLOGY IN GENERAL

ONE is under no necessity to-day of offering an apology for Biblical Theology. Divers trends of thought have combined to give it an importance and an interest which is sure to come to popular recognition. The prevalent revulsion from metaphysical dogmatism has encouraged in Christian thought a return to *authority*, in one or another form; — and by no means least to the Apostolic norm in the New Testament Canon. Authority may seem a strange term to use in connection with the distinctively modern appreciation of the New Testament Scripture, but it actually is as an authority that it is regarded, if only in the historical sense, as the unique record of the faith of the first generation of Christians. The distinction of modern Biblical study from this point of view has been that instead of seeking corroboration in the Biblical text for the separate propositions of the current church theology, it has been peculiarly open to the influence of the modern historical method, and ready to recognise that our sacred books are as well worthy as any others of the rigid scrutiny with which we have learned to interpret all historical texts.

General Recognition of Biblical Theology

The diversity however of the influences which have encouraged the study of this subject has contributed to render vague and various the conceptions of its scope and aim. Of definitions there is a lack; but from the character of the numerous books which have been issued under this name, one may infer that prevalent notions of Biblical Theology are loose enough to include at the one end a systematic theology which is marked by copious employment of Biblical texts, and at the other, a mere exegetical study of separate words and ideas.

Vagueness of Conception

No doubt in the study of any subject, and particularly in the inception of a study, there must be differences of treatment corresponding to the various degrees of completeness — rather incompleteness — at which the study has arrived. At this date we must be thankful for many studies which are partial and subsidiary. It is, however, a just ground of complaint that many works which go under the name of Biblical Theology have nothing whatever to do with it, and implicitly belie its ideal. The ideal of Biblical Theology is nevertheless capable of being defined with perfect precision and in a way which can hardly be subject to difference of opinion.

Definition of Biblical Theology

It is not a rectification of systematic theology; for systematic theology revised is systematic theology still, and neither clashes with nor coincides with the new and intermediate discipline in question. Neither is it a study of Biblical words and ideas in severalty; nor a mere topical arrangement of the results of such studies.

What it is not

It stands midway between exegesis and systematic theology. It clings very closely to the form of Biblical conceptions and at the same time strives to comprehend them in terms of a system. Its special mark is this, that it studies separately the several Biblical documents in relation to the individual authors, with the aim of reproducing the theological standpoint of each writer. The only postulate we have to demand is one which cannot readily be refused: it is, that no two men think precisely alike; but under the same terms they understand different things, and under different terms, the same thing; — that the common Apostolic doctrine was by the individual authors at least distributed in different ways, expressed under various terms, and with different emphasis. This, however, in no wise prejudices the fact that there is a substantial unity of doctrine throughout the New Testament; and it is by the method of Biblical Theology alone that such a fact can be established. An idea can be comprehended only as a part of a system, the study of an author's thought as a whole throws back a flood of light upon the several items of exegetical inquiry, and it is in this that Biblical Theology attains its characteristic expression.

<small>It is Exposition in Terms of a System</small>

In characterising Biblical Theology as an historical study we define it on two sides. In the first place, it is not directly interested in the bearing of the Biblical truths upon the religious life; it is history, not homily. The truth or falsehood, the moral value, of Biblical doctrine cannot for one moment be a matter of indifference; but in this study we are concerned simply to learn what

<small>An Historical Study</small>

was the meaning of the author. In the second place, it does not seek to go beyond the historical standpoint of the author, to extract universally valid propositions, to extend by inference — no matter with how faultless a logic — the sphere of his ideas, nor to subject his conceptions to the unity of an alien system. It does not aim to go one jot beyond the circle of ideas native to the consciousness of the writer; it does not seek to translate the author into equivalent modes of modern thought; but to interpret him in terms of his own philosophic method.

The sources with which Biblical Theology has to deal in constructing the theological doctrine of the various Biblical authors are of course primarily the genuine writings (and reported speeches) of the author. But inasmuch as these sources are in the form of history or epistle, in which the theological material is occasional, and for the most part subordinate to a hortatory aim, they are not available for our purpose so simply and directly as were they systematic theological treatises; and the theological data which they furnish are rarely abundant enough to define the author's position on all sides. For our construction we are therefore dependent in no inconsiderable degree upon such sources of information as reveal the phases of contemporary thought with which the author was in touch. Chief among these are of course the Hebrew Scriptures, with their contemporary Judaic interpretation, as being in fact the chief ground of the unity which underlies the diversity of New Testament doctrinal forms. One can hardly overestimate the importance of the Old Testament

Method of Study

Sources

as the matrix of Christian doctrine; and any study which fails to give due weight to this consideration is sure to be astray. Hardly second in importance are the New Testament Scriptures as a whole. Whatever of individuality we may find in an author, we are at least equally bound to recognise the common factor of Apostolic doctrine. Each man wrote in the Church and for the Church, assuming a comprehension and a reception of his teaching on the basis of the common faith. It is a question for Biblical Theology to settle rather than to assume, whether besides the individualities of the several authors there are to be discovered distinct schools of thought within the Apostolic period. But it is certain at least that the strongly marked individuality of S. Paul was not without influence upon his associates; and we must expect to find differences in the forms of conception of the several authors corresponding to their dependence upon Hebraic or Hellenic modes of thought. How far Hellenic philosophy, or the speculations of Hellenistic Judaism, may throw light upon New Testament doctrinal systems, is an open question. The attempt, however, in any large sense to derive New Testament doctrine from Greek philosophy is egregiously unhistorical; — if for no other reason, because of the difference of the problems in which they were interested. That the Greek stress was upon metaphysics and the Christian upon religion is a fact patent: but the further difference is to be noted that even the Greek religion was expressed in terms of ethics, while the Christian ethics was expressed in terms of theology. But the language of the New Testament is Greek, and this fact of itself, besides requiring extended lexical study in Greek sources, raises the question how far the Greek language, which was the product as well as the instrument of Greek philosophy, may have influenced the formal development of New Testament thought. It is moreover important to recognise that our New Testament Scriptures were formulated in an age in which Greek culture was disseminated throughout the world, which therefore was distinguished, in a degree to which no subsequent age has attained, by clear thought and right reason.

Biblical Theology, although in many respects it proceeds upon a new principle of interpretation, is not under the necessity of beginning the study of the Bible *de novo*. The rich heritage of the faithful study of past ages is the basis upon which alone our present development is possible, and its fruits are directly available for our purpose. The great exegetical commentaries are the chief reliance of Biblical Theology; the few which have been written with this aim specially in view have of course a more immediate value. The acute historical studies of this century in the developments of the Apostolic age have a still more lively bearing upon our subject. And as the most immediate helps we must count the numerous special studies in New Testament doctrine, most of which are more or less in line with our conception, taking account of the diversity of doctrinal types.

<small>**Helps**</small>

But the characteristic labour of Biblical Theology begins where the helps cease. Biblical Theology is essentially constructive; it rises from the close inspection of single texts to an apprehension of the author's thought as a whole.

<small>**Construction**</small>

Minute and patient exegetical study is indispensable; but no less necessary and more characteristic of this study is the broader view, the imaginative faculty checked by the historic sense, by the aid of which the scattered details are co-ordinated in a constructive reproduction of the author's thought. Both of these labours constantly interact; there is a perpetual back and forth, a comparison of text with text, of hypothesis with proof, of the particular with the general; and out of this labour grows Biblical Theology, with its representation which is at least an approximation to the lively unity of the author's thought.

It is manifestly impracticable to carry the reader through this elaborate study. Following the well known maxim that the order of instruction is the opposite of the order of investigation, the signs of labour must in the main be expunged from the face of the treatment; — the results only appear, and they are in a sense the proof of their own validity, in so far as they demonstrate themselves adequate to explain and to harmonise the author's characteristic ideas. The process of study may be allowed to appear only so far as may be necessary to the understanding of the point of view. Intelligibility must be the key-note of exposition.

Method of Exposition

SPECIAL PROBLEMS INVOLVED IN THE STUDY OF THE DOCTRINE OF S. JOHN

THE study of each author meets us with special problems of its own, depending upon the extent and character of the literary sources, upon their date, and upon the possible affinities of the writer. It is manifestly a more difficult matter to determine the theological position of such men as S. Peter, or S. James, or S. Luke; than that, for instance, of S. Paul, in whom the logical faculty came to clearer expression, and whose writings, not only by reason of their greater compass, but by the very fact of their predominant controversial character, give a sharper definition to his theology.

Problems peculiar to each Author

There are certain widely accepted claims in respect to the date and the philosophical affinities of the Johannine writings which must be carefully weighed in the course of study, but which, in so far as they are not adopted, cannot without prejudice to clearness and unity come to expression in the finished exposition. Nevertheless we shall see in the course of the treatment that the marked predilection which has been shown for S. John by the Mystics and kindred thinkers is due in part to a misinterpretation of his thought. The contention that he manifests a type of thought akin to the Platonic realism — whether independent or derived — can only be misleading. There is a trait

Date and Affinities of S. John

which we may denominate the Johannine idealism; but it is of a Hebrew, not of a Greek mould. The claim that the Epistle of S. John, or the Gospel, or both, exhibit the influence of the Gnosticism of the second century has been discredited by the fanciful procedure of its adherents; and we shall see that the so-called dualism which is so prominent a trait of the Johannine writings is of a very different character and suggests a widely different explanation. Not so readily can we dispose of the claim that the Johannine writings show substantial dependence upon the thought of Hellenic Judaism; of the apparent Antijudaism of the Gospel; or of the Tübingen hypothesis which, ever seeking a "tendency," finds in S. John's Gospel the purpose of expressing the life of Christ in harmony with the regnant gentile catholicism of the second century. These questions must come to consideration in the course of the essay; and in particular, the problem of the relation of S. John to Philo will be treated in connection with the Logos idea, where it will be seen how slight is the clew which has led into this path. It cannot fairly be considered a proof of prejudice that one abides by the traditional account of the authorship and date of the Johannine writings. At all events the traditional hypothesis like every other must be judged by its fitness to explain the phenomena of the writings in question, — and of all the writings.

When we consider the Johannine sources (the Gospel, the three Epistles, and the Revelation) with reference to their value for Biblical Theology, the first question is not whether they are genuine, but whether they may

Character and Value of the Johannine Sources

be ascribed to a common author. The question of genuineness is one which is rather to be proved than **Genuineness** posited by Biblical Theology. For it must be evident that these documents, be they written when or by whom they may, furnish data for the determination of the writer's thought, and that on this interpretation depends in part the decision of the authorship. Biblical Theology would lose its apologetic value were it to assume what it is in a position to prove. Nevertheless the claim of perfect impartiality upon such a point as this is a vain boast. The Johannine authorship of the Fourth Gospel is the most vital question of New Testament criticism; here if anywhere is the line which divides a rationalising interpretation of Christianity from one which can in any sense be called orthodox. With this question we decide whether among those who heard, who saw with their eyes, who beheld, and handled with their hands, we have any witness that the person of Jesus impressed in such wise his familiar companions that they recognised him as God: — not in the easy fashion of a polytheism which deified every emperor, but in the sense of the exalted Hebrew monotheism in which they were bred. It is marvellous to note how certain schools of thought, without even raising the question of Johannine authorship, reconstruct their Christianity upon a basis which is valid only in the case of its negation. But however the issue may be obscured, it is this question which must decide in the last resort how we are to regard the central fact of Christianity. For if S. John wrote, it is not possible to say that the genius of S. Paul foisted upon the church a conception of Christ which was strange to the original Apostles. If S. John testified to beholding in the humble manifestation of Jesus "a Glory as of the only begotten of the Father"; then is there a flaw in the numerous "lives of Jesus" which, on the basis of a critical selection out of the synoptic accounts, represent his earthly manifestation as "emptied" of all traits of divinity which might inspire the thought that he was more than man. About the decision of such a question hosts of presuppositions gather, and not the least is the presumption that one who had known Jesus as a man could not believe him to be God. If in a question of so great moment Biblical Theology may not furnish the decisive settlement, it can at least declare the bearing of the internal evidence *pro* or *con*. And this essay, so far as its apologetic bearing is concerned, has at the very least a value in rebuttal, and sets a *nihil obstat* upon the claim of Apostolic authorship. The hypothesis that the author was the Galilean disciple of Jesus, the "pillar" of the Jerusalem church, the venerable "presbyter" of the churches of Asia Minor, is not however to be judged merely upon its own merits, but in connection with a criticism of the opposing hypotheses which reveals their relative unfitness.

The acknowledgment of the common authorship of the Gospel and the Epistles (or rather the patent fact which renders denial trivial) contributes much to the simplicity of our task. This already provides us with material which in compass is greater than the writings of any other of the New Testament authors except those of S. Matthew, S. Luke and S. Paul; and is exceeded by S. Paul alone in the abundance of its information upon the writer's theological standpoint. It is this sufficiency of unquestionable material which renders the question of the genuineness of the Apocalypse one of secondary — at least not vital — importance to Biblical Theology. The authorship of the Apocalypse is so widely disputed, and the question is altogether one of so great difficulty, that it would seriously impair the value of the study of S. John's theology to assume its genuineness. It is generally admitted that the Apocalypse differs so widely in style and in religious outlook from the other Johannine writings as to make it exceedingly difficult to conceive how they could have been produced by a common author. On the other hand the points of resemblance are so marked that even those who deny the genuineness of both are compelled to derive them from a common school of thought. It is not difficult to imagine that, with the difference in date which we may readily assume, and with some new light upon the genesis, aim, and meaning of the Apocalypse, the contrarieties which now arrest our judgment may be dissipated. Biblical Theology may conduce to this result by proving a fundamental agreement in theological conception: but it can do this only by maintaining its independence and by studying each document for itself.

When we compare the Johannine writings with those of S. Paul, we notice that whereas the latter, **S. John's Writings a Normal Expression** by reason of their predominantly controversial character define more precisely the author's position; the writings of S. John, by the fact that they are developed without controversy, with a normal, natural emphasis and direction, have a value for the purposes of Biblical Theology which is hardly if at all inferior. This characteristic of S. John's writings is certainly not due to any lack of appreciation of the errors which threatened the Church, or of readiness to oppose them (witness the first part of the Revelation and the practical admonitions of the Epistle); but probably to the fact that S. John was not equipped for controversy; — denunciation, "fire from heaven," was his rôle. He knew but one way to oppose error, and that was to state the truth — fully, with all the majesty that it assumed in his own contemplation — and let it work. Behind the Johannine writings we seem to feel as it were the presence of a world power which is able to oppress the Church, not only by physical violence, but by spiritual delusion: but all the attempts that have been made to represent the Johannine writings as expressly formulated to controvert one or another form of error, are wrecked upon the fact that the author's expressions have nowhere the precision of reference which we must expect in such a case, and most of all from a man of so downright and ardent a disposition as he manifests. The importance of this peculiarity for the purpose of our study cannot be overestimated; it assures us that we have no casual or imperfect representation, no colouring nor warping of the exposition under the influence of a transitory interest; but an expression of S. John's native and inmost thought developed with perfect spontaneity from the depths of his intuitional and emotional nature.

There is however another feature of the Johannine writings which appears at first sight to be an effectual stumbling-block in the way of our study of S. John's doctrine. The Gospel which is by far our most abundant source is in the form of a history, and purports to give, not primarily S. John's doctrine, but the teaching of Jesus. If therefore we are to maintain in any sense the authenticity of the reported speeches of Jesus, it seems as though we must be restricted, for the special purpose of our study, to the mere comments of the author, which constitute a relatively insignificant part of his work. This, however, is a problem which is by no means so difficult of solution, nor so open to controversy, as might be imagined. The question of the historicity of the speeches of Jesus in the Fourth Gospel, vital as it is for the religious interest, is not one of immediate concern to Biblical Theology: we are here exclusively concerned with the doctrines of the *writer*. But without the least prejudice to the substantial authenticity of these reports, it takes but slight attention to the subject, but slight familiarity with the contrast between the Synoptic Gospels and S. John's, to convince one that they are not *verbatim* reports, that in form at least they reflect the peculiarities of S. John, who puts, not only in the mouth of Jesus, but of the Baptist and of the Jews, the same characteristic language which we find him employing in his Epistle; — to realise in short that the speeches of Jesus contain only what S. John had completely assimilated and made his own, and that the Fourth Gospel is, as we call it, the Gospel *according to S. John*.

<small>The Gospel as a Source of S. John's Theology</small>

Thus the Gospel is vindicated as a source of prime importance for the study of the Johannine theology.

The very character and arrangement of the composition, the aim and the scope of it, also furnish data of the very highest value for the determination of the author's theological standpoint. Here we are already entering upon the theme of the next chapter, in which we pass from these preliminaries to the exposition proper.

GENERAL CHARACTERISTICS OF S. JOHN'S THOUGHT

GENERAL CHARACTERISTICS OF S. JOHN'S THOUGHT

WE are able even from a general survey to make some highly important deductions in regard to the characteristic theological standpoint of the author.

The Outstanding Features of the Writings Reveal the Fundamental Characteristics of the Author

One of our most important problems, one which serves more than any other to fix the place of the author and the prevailing emphasis of his thought, is that in regard to the aim of his Gospel.

Aim of the Gospel

The proposition that the author of the Fourth Gospel was acquainted with our Synoptists, though it is one which — to use an expression of Jeremy Taylor's — has "more truth than evidence on its side," is nevertheless so generally accepted that, without going aside from our purpose to argue it out, we must estimate its significance for our conception of S. John's Gospel. Proceeding from this consideration, men often draw certain very serious and by no means harmonious deductions with regard to the aim of S. John's work. Now the first thing which strikes one in the comparison of S. John's Gospel with the Synoptists, is their *difference*, both in form and in material. What then was the relation of the author to these earlier authorities? Manifestly he was not bent like S. Luke 1 1-3 upon compiling a

Acquaintance with the Synoptists

Correction, or Supplement

history from various sources; it is his sovereign independence which is the most noteworthy fact in this connection. His aloofness amazes us. Now and again we think we detect an allusion to, an explanation or correction of, a Synoptic incident, yet so elusive is it that only in the rarest cases can we attain any confidence that the definite account was before his mind. Yet all the while we know that both he and his readers were familiar with several accounts of the Lord's life, some of which were held in singular veneration; and we find him relying upon this current information to such an extent that the omissions of his Gospel constitute a very notable feature of it. The birth in Bethlehem, the Davidic genealogy, the Baptism, the Temptation, the Transfiguration, the *Pater noster*, the institution of Baptism, the Last Supper, and the Ascension, are not recorded by S. John. Some however are indirectly alluded to and others plainly presupposed; and at all events it is scarcely claimed any longer that S. John's omissions are implicit denials. If we take note of the points which seem to be corrections in minor detail of the traditional account, as for instance the date of the Crucifixion, they are revealed so incidentally as to be practically ineffective for correction and quite inadequate to constitute the author's set aim. It is moreover commonly conceded that the impression which the Gospel makes of unity of design, the stamp of a single moulding principle, precludes the idea that the form of its development was subordinated to a purpose of incidental correction or supplement. But what if the work were intended to traverse, not incidentally, but in principle, the Synoptic representation of Jesus? Manifestly, if it were an Apostle who found this course necessary, he could not in any honesty have refrained from explicit denunciation of the false tradition. But what if it were rather a philosopher of a later age who wished to coin a representation of Jesus' life more in harmony with the developed doctrine of the Church, but precisely on account of his lack of authority dare not break openly with the venerated tradition? So far as regards the particular point at issue this might be admitted a plausible explanation. But then it is observed (and here is one of the turning points of the criticism) that, both in detail, and in the general account of the course and significance of events, the author displays an exactness of information which is inconceivable in a dreamer of the second century. This throws a strong light upon the question of the author's authority and upon the reliableness of his representation as a whole. Of such traits, the most commonly acknowledged is the representation of repeated attendance upon the feasts at Jerusalem, with the consequent prolongation of Jesus' ministry and of his activity in Jerusalem in particular. Without this hint the development of the history recorded in the Synoptists is not readily conceivable. To meet this it is suggested that the author, though not S. John, was an immediate disciple who wrote out of the fulness of his reminiscence of the Apostle's teaching. But we can at least say that this sovereign attitude toward the tradition looks *as if* it pointed to an author who, in the confidence of his personal and intimate witness of the facts which he had " seen " and " heard " and " handled," could not feel cumbered about the prepotence of any external authority; who rather wrote at a time when he was weighted with the consciousness that beside himself,

> "there is left on earth
> No one alive who knew (consider this) —
> Saw with his eyes and handled with his hands
> That which was from the first the Word of Life."

Supplement in some sense was the aim, for a supplement the Gospel practically is: but it is precisely in regard to the motive of this supplement that we are interested. The aim was not the presentation of specific new material, for that end would have been more simply accomplished by adhering to the scheme of the Synoptic account. It did not claim to complete the record of the events of Jesus' life, for the author naïvely confesses that "there are also many other things which Jesus did, the which if they should be written every one, I suppose that even the world itself would not contain the books that should be written 21 ²⁵.

We approach the solution when we note that the material is *selected* with particular design. The incidents recorded are fewer than in the Synoptic accounts, but they are narrated in more detail and with more appreciation of both their pragmatic and their dogmatic significance. The miracles are not only different, but greater; and not only greater (in the sense of manifesting more clearly the exercise of supernatural power), but peculiarly adapted — according to S. John's constant and express point of view — to serve as "signs"; — that is, not only as legitimations of Jesus' mission, but as manifestations of its character.

Every consideration leads us to conclude that the aim of the Gospel is accurately represented in S. John's own declaration: "Many other signs therefore did Jesus in the presence of the disciples, which are not written in this book; but these are written that ye may believe that Jesus is the Christ, the Son of God; and that believing ye may have life in his name" 20 30 31. This valuation of Jesus' miracles is particularly expressed in relation to that "beginning of signs" which he did in Cana of Galilee, which served to manifest his glory and encourage the faith of his disciples 2 11. But it is not only Jesus' signs; it is also his teaching which has in the Fourth Gospel a special reference to his Person. Jesus' self-witness is nowhere else so constant, so clear and so lofty. To this difference in the content of Jesus' teaching corresponds a difference of form which hints at its explanation. It is commonly remarked that along with the other notes of difference which characterise the speeches of Jesus in the Fourth Gospel, with the absence of the clear-minted gnomic utterances which were so eminently adapted for oral transmission, there fails too the parabolic mode of teaching which was the most notable distinction of Jesus' discourses according to the Synoptists. Nevertheless there is an abundance of lively natural imagery in S. John, and it would be nearer the truth to say that in S. John we have the parable elucidated and explained, as it was in Jesus' esoteric instruction of the disciples. That there was an esoteric trait in Jesus' teaching, meant only for the closer disciples, is clearly expressed in the Synoptic ac-

A Representation of the Significance of Jesus' Person is the Mark of the Gospel

count, Matt. 13 ¹⁰. The parables were for the people, "the mysteries of the kingdom of heaven" only for the disciples. S. John's representation then is to this effect, that the preponderance of Jesus' teaching was with regard to his own Person: what he was, and what men must believe about him. But S. John carries this esoteric trend even further; for, as he sees in the saying of Caiaphas 11 ₄₉₋₅₂ a prophecy which was quite aside from the conscious meaning of the speaker, so in the speeches of Jesus he reads a meaning which even the Apostles themselves did not divine at the time 7 ₃₉. More remarkable still however, and more significant, is the fact that the whole character of the representation, the general scheme of the Gospel, is designed to bear upon this very point. Everything is made to hinge upon the appreciation or rejection of Jesus, upon belief or disbelief in him, upon men's ability to see, or their blindness to God's manifestation in him.

All of these considerations unite in representing that the aim of S. John's Gospel was a higher char-

The Teaching of a Higher Significance of Christ's Person is the Aim of the Gospel

acterisation of the significance of Christ's person. In the first place, it was higher than his own earlier appreciation, for "that Jesus is the Christ," in 20 ₃₁, is doubtless a confession of much deeper import than the identical confession of S. Peter recorded in Matt. 16 ₁₆, and "Son of God" means more than is represented in the genealogy of S. Luke. Not only was the Resurrection a crisis for the disciples' appreciation of Jesus, but S. John doubtless through all the years of his life grew to fuller and fuller comprehension of the profound words and mighty deeds of which he was witness. In fact this development in appreciation of the truth, and particularly of the truth concerning Jesus, is an idea persistently reiterated in S. John's Gospel in connection with the mission of the Comforter 14 ^{26} 15 ^{26} 16 $^{12-14}$. And in S. John's reminiscence, "I have yet many things to say unto you, but ye cannot bear them now," "He shall glorify me, for he taketh of mine, and shall declare it unto you," we read his own consciousness of a life spent in learning, of a long period of spiritual guidance which had taught him to see all acquisitions of truth in their reference to Jesus, and to value them as they conduced to glorify him. In the second place, his characterisation of Jesus' Person was higher, not than the belief current in the Church (for he shows no consciousness of writing against prevailing opposition, and the very term Logos is introduced without explanation, as a thing familiar at least to the circle of readers immediately in view); not higher than the standpoint of the writers of the Synoptic Gospels (witness S. Luke's relation to S. Paul): but higher than the prevailing *representation*, and supplemental to it in precisely this respect.

The characteristic difference between the Synoptic Gospels and the Fourth Gospel, which is so often accounted to the discredit of the latter, is explained simply by the fact that S. John's Gospel alone was composed by a companion of the Lord. That the Gospels of S. Luke and of S. Mark were not written by "those who from the beginning were eye-witnesses and ministers of the word," is expressly declared by the one and assumed in the very name of the other.

The Fourth Gospel alone composed by an Eye-witness

There is also in the Gospel of S. Matthew no single trait, far less an explicit claim, to distinguish it, in respect to its character and origin, from the other two; and the modern critical theory, which is accepted almost as widely as the historical method itself, and in this instance is accordant with early tradition, posits an employment of literary (or oral) sources by all the Synoptists alike. There are grave difficulties in the way of a concordant estimate of the nature of these sources; but that the Synoptic accounts as we now have them were dependent upon sources, single or sundry, written or oral, and were in this sense secondary, is a matter of general agreement. It is worth while to linger a moment upon this subject that we may glean such credit as it suggests for S. John's Gospel. Now between the account compiled by one who had no personal experience of the recorded events, and that of an eye-witness, there is an essential difference. This is not necessarily, as it is often assumed, a difference of historical accuracy, but of independence. The speeches of Jesus which are recorded in the Synoptic Gospels are in a sense their own legitimation: quite apart from the confirmation the Gospels receive from their acceptance by the Church, no one will dispute that they represent substantially, and even with formal accuracy, the character of Jesus' teaching. These sententious, gnomic utterances, these familiar parables, were not only peculiarly adapted to take the attention of the people; but in a degree only equalled by rhythmic forms they were also suited for accurate oral transmission. Such sayings as readily riveted themselves upon the memory, such as were most readily intelligible to the people, which must therefore have formed the staple of Apostolic preaching; — such, and such alone, could have constituted the oral Gospels which probably preceded the written. It is in the highest degree creditable to the faithfulness of the Evangelists that they remain throughout subservient to the authority of their sources: it cannot be claimed that they have coloured the speeches of Jesus from their individual standpoints, at the most one can infer their own peculiarities of thought from their selection and arrangement of their material. We can imagine that had S. John written a diary it would have been found similar to the Synoptic account in this respect, that the words and deeds would have been recorded with simple objectivity and with precisely that degree of appreciation which they in fact received at the time; though even in that case there would have been an emphasis upon the things which seemed specially significant to him. But S. John's Gospel is something very different from a diary; something different, too, from mere story-telling. It has been claimed that this Gospel is not a history but a philosophy; and with a certain amount of truth, for his account is not chiefly interested in the narration of events, but in the significance which they had with respect to Christ. Written, as is universally assumed, in his extreme old age, it represents what the Gospel had then come to mean to him, and what he would have all men understand it to mean. He had a certain liberal disregard of formal accuracy, which was due to his consciousness that all that he had learnt was from Christ, that his teaching was Christ's teaching, and that he consequently could not misrepresent the truth, as he strove to exposit, in his own terms and to a generation which stood already far both in time and place from the facts which he relates, the central significance of the manifestation of him who was the Christ, the Son of God. I shall struggle no longer to picture the standpoint from which S. John wrote, for Robert Browning has done it with rare historic insight in " A Death in the Desert."

> " Since much that at the first, in deed and word,
> Lay simply and sufficiently exposed,
> Had grown (or else my soul was grown to match,
> Fed through such years, familiar with such light,
> Guarded and guided still to see and speak)
> Of new significance and fresh result;
> What first were guessed as points, I now knew stars,
> And named them in the Gospel I have writ."

He would have all others see as he saw, confident that his vision was no subjective idealisation; but that, however he himself may have failed in that earlier day to see, the truth was nevertheless there manifested in objective reality, and only because men were blind did they fail to see, only because they were deaf did they fail to hear.

> "Then stand before that fact, that Life and Death,
> Stay there at gaze, till it dispart, dispread,
> As though a star should open out, all sides,
> Grow the world on you, as it is my world."

This considerable excursion into the province of Biblical criticism is only justifiable inasmuch as it has **Subjective and Objective** brought to notice many of the peculiarities of S. John's Gospel which must be kept in view, and in especial the relation of his thought to the Person of Christ which is the most outstanding moment of his doctrinal presentation. This line of thought leads us directly to the consideration of another characteristic of a general nature without which the organisation of S. John's thought must be incomprehensible, or at least self-conflicting. This is the fact that together with a preponderating representation of the subjective significance of Christ's manifestation (according to which the revelation of God in Christ seems to be of itself sufficient for the accomplishment of salvation) S. John contends most emphatically for the objective reality of the things narrated. It seems at first sight as though he were interested only in the moral effectiveness of the revelation; but again it is " that which we have heard, that which we have seen with our eyes, and our hands have handled," and the orthodox confession is " that Jesus Christ is come in the flesh." This is not the manner of a man who stands far from the event and is solely concerned with its philosophical or ethical importance. The comparison with S. Paul is instructive in this connection. For him also the objective reality of the great dogmatic facts of Christ's life is of essential importance: but the difference lies in this, that whereas S. Paul in accordance with his analytic genius abstracts the dogmatic moment from the lively unity of its personal and ethical connection (it is the death and the resurrection of Christ which are the indispensable basis of his dogmatic scheme), S. John has ever before his eye the life of Jesus as a whole, and finds in it at one and the same moment the basis of dogmatic inference (its objective importance), and its subjective value as the highest revelation. It is for this reason that he regards the Incarnation as the prime fact, precisely because it is the most inclusive category. It is not that S. John's emphasis lay upon the Incarnation in the narrower sense, as a particular moment in Jesus' career (his birth, the inception of his life); or as a separable dogma, contrasted for instance with his Death. "The Word became flesh" I 14 is rather (like "coming" I 9, "manifested" I. 1 2 and "sent" I. 4 14) an expression for the total manifestation of Christ (birth, life, death, and resurrection); and serves at once to denote a dogmatic fact and to express the significance of Christ as the Revealer of God I 18. This characteristic of S. John runs through and through his representation, and the failure to take account of it is largely responsible for the common though erroneous opinion that the Death, the Resurrection, and the Ascension of Christ have no dogmatic importance in the Fourth Gospel. It is unquestionable that the prevailing emphasis of S. John is upon the subjective appropriation of salvation through the revelation of the truth, and it seems at times 6 63 as though in this interest he were bent upon rationalising the objective facts of Christ's life. The fact is however that these two ranges of ideas subsist side by side without the least consciousness on the part of the writer of any contrast, far less of any contradiction, between them.

S. John's treatment of the "works" of Jesus throws light upon his conception of Jesus' Work in the greater sense. The miraculous works of Jesus, S. John calls "signs"; and not only by this name, but by his constant representation, he reveals his conception of them as expressions of Christ's mission, and that in a double character: as wonders, exceeding the limits of natural force, they legitimate his mission as from God 3 ²; as symbols they reveal the character of his mission 6 ². In the first point of view it is the greatness of the miracle which is significant 5 ²⁰ 7 ³¹; in the second, it is its kind 10 ³². The resurrection of Lazarus owes its importance not merely to its character as a wonder, but to the fact that it manifests Jesus as the Resurrection and the Life. Similarly the healing of the blind man brings out the idea of light, the feeding of the multitude, the idea of bread, and the beginning of signs in Cana surely owes its significance as a manifestation of his glory to something more than the mere natural impossibility of the wonder,—it reveals in fact the contrast between the attitude of Jesus and the traditional position of Israel; between the regime of ceremonial purification (to which John the Baptist still belonged), and the glad life-giving wine of the Gospel. All the signs of Jesus serve to manifest in visible and earthly form the character of his work in the more real though invisible sphere. But the idea that "the signs" are for S. John merely symbolical representations of the thought contained in Jesus' word, leaves out of consideration the fact that with even greater emphasis he denominates them "*works*." As signs, Jesus' works are practically words; but it must not be overlooked that word and work are constantly contrasted, that each is in a certain sense the supplement of the other, each being in its own special way a ground of faith. The significance of Jesus' miracles lies very essentially in this, that they represent works wrought, as well as truth taught. A mere talking Christ does not help the world; the Son therefore manifests himself (and also reveals the Father) as a *worker* 5 17. The "works" have for S. John a special importance, distinguished from that of the "words" in this, that they reveal the will and the might to perform that which is promised in the "word." Therefore it is not the speech but the deed of Christ which is essentially the ground of faith; — "if I do not *do*, believe me not" 10 37. The "word" is a ground of faith only in so far as it includes in itself the assurance that the "work" will follow, and this confidence it rightly evokes because it comes from God. The Father not only speaks, but he "doeth his works" 14 10.

In another aspect however the "word" is raised in dignity above the "work"; and that not only because it brings to expression more perfectly than the material sign the significance of Jesus' Person and promise; but because precisely as *word* it belongs to a higher sphere, is namely "spirit" 6 64, whereas the work considered merely as a wonder belongs to the earthly sphere and is "flesh." It is from this point of view that the insufficiency of the sign as a motive of faith is frequently emphasised. "Flesh," the sphere in which the sign is wrought, has not with S. John any connotation of evil, of sin; it is simply unprofitable 6 63, — flesh generates only flesh and cannot raise itself to the sphere of spirit 3 6. It cannot however be supposed that in 6 63, Jesus means to cast discredit upon the miracle of the loaves, for it was a work of God though wrought in the earthly sphere, it was also a sign and hence in a sense a word; — thought wedding itself to fact. Spirit and flesh, elsewhere contrasted, here become one; each of

Jesus' works is an epitome of his Work in its totality, for in each is exemplified the Word becoming flesh. We can thus see how it is that the works of Jesus have at one and the same time and inseparably the significance of a deed done in all objective actuality, and of a revelation whose importance lies in its subjective appreciation.

This helps us to understand the constant blending — we cannot say confusion — of subjective and objective, which may be observed in S. John's treatment of Jesus' " Work" 17 4 in the greater sense. The same passage, chapter 6, serves as a transition to this subject. As Jesus' words in verse 63 cannot be supposed to disallow the divine significance of his miracle; neither can they be considered an attempt to rationalise the " hard saying." If eating his flesh meant nothing more than accepting the revelation contained in his teaching, there would have been left in this saying no cause of stumbling. The real and objective importance of Christ's descent from heaven 6 38, his death 6 51, and his ascension 6 62, is not nullified by the fact that they are at the same time vehicles of revelation and in this sense have the same significance (quickening, spiritual, life-giving) as the words that he speaks. In the hard saying 6 52-59 about the eating of his flesh we are compelled to recognise — quite apart from its obvious association with the sacrament of the Last Supper — a reference to his death in terms of *sacrifice*, and after every attempt has been made to rationalise it in terms of revelation and spiritual communion, there must remain a residuum of absolutely objective character; — or else Jesus made use of an expression which was needlessly offensive to his disciples. It was not the eating of his flesh in objective reality, which was stigmatised as unprofitable, and opposed to the spirit; but the blind ignorance of the people who could not see in his words the profound spiritual idea of sacrifice. In saying, "The words that I have spoken unto you are spirit, and are life," he cannot be supposed to be explaining a sentence which was imperfect and enigmatical; but in the most solemn way, and in the face of misunderstanding, he bears witness to the foregoing words as the perfect and ultimate expression of truth; — for the words which are spirit and life are none other than these, "Except ye eat the flesh of the Son of man and drink his blood, ye have not life in yourselves."

S. John in every individual moment of Jesus' life and in his total manifestation sees these two factors, word and work; and though he distinguishes them, he never thinks of them as separable. They stood in a relation of contrast; and yet the work was in a sense a word, and the word, a work. That Christ's word was at all times a work was a conception very essential to S. John. It was suggested by the creative word in the first chapter of Genesis, and was thus immediately connected with his use of the term Logos in the prologue. The power of Christ's word is seen not only in the performance of his miracles, but in the fact that it was a powerfully efficient and life-giving revelation. And so the word wrought and the work taught, and yet each was a distinct factor essentially irreducible to the terms of the other, though both became one in the Incarnation of the Logos. Of these two factors, it was doubtless the word, the idea of revelation, upon which S. John predominantly dwelt; but both are to be felt often where only one is expressed, and neither can be counted to nullify the other. How naïve was S. John's mode of thought may be seen sufficiently from one example: "Herein was the love of God manifested in us ... that he sent his Son the propitiation for our sins" I. 4 9 10. Here in accord with S. John's constant conception the significance of Christ's coming (sending) into the world, and in particular of his death, lay largely in the revelation which was thereby made of God's love; and yet the death of Christ remains none the less a *propitiation*, and quite apart from any subjective apprehension of it, he views it as the propitiatory sacrifice " also for the sins of the whole world" I. 2 2.

It has been necessary to dwell so long on this point because it is precisely here that S. John is most commonly and fatally misinterpreted. S. John's doctrine cannot be evaporated into a mere subjective system of revelation, faith, knowledge, life; it grasps the mere fact, *the flesh*, and finds in it a significance which is not to be ignored because, as a mystery transcending the understanding, it is not a frequent topic of the exposition. If this were not so, we should indeed be obliged to ascribe the Johannine writings to a speculative genius of the second century, who stood far from the facts, and valued only the moral effectiveness of the tale. We should be forced to admit that a Palestinian Jew could not have strayed so far from the pragmatic postulates of his inherited faith. But with the appreciation we have just gained of S. John's mode of thought we may perceive that so far from its being the reflection of a philosopher, it is the intuition of an eye-witness which best serves to explain this characteristic blending of subjective and objective in a unity, which is nothing else than the unity of a person. The Person of Christ was for S. John the grand fact, which he estimated on all sides, but did not analyse. With this characteristic of the Johannine writings the historical situation of the Apostle John is not only in no way inconsistent; we may rather say that such a situation is demanded as the only adequate explanation of the facts.

There are many other characteristics of the Johannine writings which are elucidated by the character, the position and the development of S. John. His early passage through the school of the Baptist to the inmost circle of Christ's followers, his gradual and spontaneous development, help in particular to explain the difference between him and S. Paul. There was for him no essential opposition between Law and Gospel; for the freedom of his early Galilean life was not crushed in Pharisaic bondage. He had learned the law from Christ, and although Jesus' attitude toward law was radically new, S. John found it natural to express the teaching of Christ, and indeed the sum of his self-revelation, as the "new commandment." He had passed through no such sudden spiritual revolution as S. Paul, and hence did not like him conceive of the conflict of good and evil as fought out within the sphere of the individual conscience. Though he recognised the opposing principles quite as vividly, he did not name them, from the standpoint of the human consciousness, Flesh and Spirit; but, in view

The Intuitional Character of S. John's Thought

of the great world drama which he beheld enacting
about him (as in the Apocalypse), Light and Darkness. The nature of S. John's thought is profoundly
contemplative and intuitional. Nothing can be further
from truth than to call him speculative. He never
speculates, he sees. He is called the Seer of the
Apocalypse; he might be called no less aptly the
Seer of the Gospel, the Seer of the Epistle. He
sees a drama: the conflict, and finally the victory, of
the powers of Light over the Darkness; and he
simply writes what he sees. He sees the earthly
manifestation of the Son of God; and he pictures it
in his Gospel:

> "To me that story — ay, that Life and Death,
> Of which I wrote 'it was,' — to me it is;
> — Is, here and now; I apprehend nought else."

He leans upon Jesus' breast, looking into the beloved
face which reveals to him the light of the Glory of
God; and in the full inspiration of that sight he turns,
in his Epistle, to impart to his brethren the practical
significance, the moral result, of that manifested life.
Logical analysis, dialectical method in general, was
quite foreign to S. John. His thought moves grandly
in the sphere of a few profound ideas the significance
of which he develops by contrast. For the antithetical expression which is so characteristic of his
writings he finds the immediate suggestion in the
parallelism of Hebrew literature. Moreover in what
seem at first to be disconnected antitheses there is a
real progression of thought, and a mode of development which, far as it is from representing a continuous
deductive sequence, has nevertheless all the formality

of a syllogism. But antithesis is for S. John far more than a literary form or a figure of speech. It is the expression of his deepest thought. He sees everything in its essential character, and hence in fundamental contrast; — not blended and mingled with its opposite as it is in phenomenal experience. The fundamental contrast between God and all that is not of God, he names according to its different aspects: Light and Darkness, Life and Death, Love and Hate. The Logos is conceived of in no theosophic manner as the mediator of this contrast; — he was manifested to destroy the works of the Devil, the Darkness is to be abolished, and is already passing away before the shining of the true Light.

S. John distinguishes between different stages of development; but he sees in the germ the potency of the fruit, and therefore eternal life is actually possessed by the believer now, though its full fruition is to be expected in the hereafter. Appreciation of Christ's Person and confidence in his might is called faith, in every stage, from the lowest to the highest, and at every stage it works eternal life because it makes that knowledge to be truly living, upon which eternal life depends; we have even now a true knowledge of God which works in us his likeness, though we shall be perfectly like him only "when we see him as he is."

S. John's ideas, not only in the Gospel but in the Epistle, cluster more closely about Christ than do those of any other writer. It may not be just to say that S. John's thought is swayed more than another's by the Christian point of view; but there is in this respect a

The Close Relation of S. John's Thought to Christ

peculiarity in his mode of thought which is best brought out by a comparison with S. Paul. This difference between S. Paul and S. John is in accord with the mental peculiarities we have already noted. S. Paul's doctrine is no less securely rooted in Christ; but he is free to move away from that central point along the chain of a dialectical argument, his thinking moves in enthymemes, and so his ideas, which are no less really attached to the centre, are attached less directly. S. John on the other hand, as we have found, simply sees and knows and tells. S. Paul can draw arguments from all sides, examples from law, inductions from history, analogies from nature; and although he converges them all upon the central truth he thereby exhibits a point of difference from S. John. S. John never moves a step away from the centre. That word which he uses with predilection to describe the close relation of the believer to Christ — " dwelleth," or " abideth," in him — might be used to describe this characteristic of his thought; it *abides* in him. When I study S. John's Epistle, I picture him leaning still upon Jesus' breast, and ever gazing into his face. If there is any question to solve, he finds the answer there. No argument is needed; — or only one step of argument, as he directly subsumes the case under the idea of the nature of God. If there is a problem raised by the lack of harmony in the brotherhood, he looks up into the face of God and in that look he knows that " he that loveth not knoweth not God, for God is love." If the brotherhood is tempted to sin, the denunciation comes with a directness and absoluteness which is simply perplexing and inconceivable except from this point of view. We see again the ardent, fiery spirit of the Son of Thunder; the same man who in the Apocalypse anathematised the lukewarm, and ever sees things in their deepest nature as contrasts. Looking into the face of Jesus, into that face which is to him the perfect revelation of the love and holiness of God, he cannot but say: "He that sinneth hath not known God." A very simple but significant illustration of the constant attachment of S. John's thought to Christ is his use in the Epistle of the pronouns He and Him (αὐτός, ἐκεῖνος) for Christ (or God), but with grammatical reference so loose that the reader is often puzzled about the syntax. It is only because it is manifest that the thought of Christ is constantly uppermost in S. John's mind that there is no real hesitancy in determining the reference of these familiar pronouns. In reading S. John's Epistle we adapt ourselves so thoroughly to his spirit that it seems in the end natural to refer to 'Him' as though He were always the subject of the preceding clause. There is however often a real difficulty in distinguishing whether the reference is to Christ or to God I. 1 5-10, though the discussion of commentators on this point is quite beside the mark, for the significance of this apparent looseness of expression is just this, that to S. John it was all the same: he knew the Father only as he was revealed in the Son, and his inmost thought was regulated by the truth which he recorded, "I and the Father are one" 10 30.

The very language of S. John reflects the simplicity of his mental processes. It also indicates his affinity with Hebrew thought; and the hint which we derive from this general consideration is confirmed by the more particular study of the relation of S. John's ideas to the Old Testament. This is a point of the utmost importance for the study of S. John, for not only does the question of authorship hinge upon it, but its appreciation affects quite radically the interpretation and construction of the Johannine theology. Depending as we must upon delicate inference for the establishment of the author's system of theology, it cannot but be of prime interest for us to know whether the background of his thought about God and the world was Hebrew or Greek. We cannot in our study proceed upon the mere assumption of the traditional view of the author's relation to Judaism; but still less dare one neglect this assumption, or without proof to the contrary, deny that which is the intended implication of the Gospel itself. In the detailed treatment of S. John's several ideas we shall notice the close relation to Old Testament conceptions, and the total impression must be that the author was bred in the atmosphere, and instinctively clothed his ideas in the forms, of Jewish thought. We have here only to remark upon the Aramaic characteristics of S. John's *style;* a more objective consideration, and one which, though it carries the main assumption with it, is less a subject of dispute.

The Aramaic Traits of S. John's Language Furnish a Hint of the Hebraic Affinities of his Thought

The consideration of linguistic peculiarities, is, in its very nature, a study too minute to be presented here with proof and reference. But the following points are obvious enough to be perceived even in the English translation. That the Gospel was written for Greek-speaking Christians is shown by the frequent explanation of Aramaic words and Hebrew customs. To this agrees the unimpeachable tradition that S. John found the later sphere of his activity in the essentially Heathen-Christian communities of Asia Minor. The Gospel was therefore *originally* written in Greek. Yet notwithstanding a certain readiness and ease in the use of the Greek tongue, which presumes a prolonged residence in Greek surroundings, one can still distinguish through the Greek dress the type of the mother tongue of the Palestinian. The most general signs of it are: the simple and unperiodic structure of the sentences; the monotonous connection of sentences by " and," " but," " then," to the neglect of the rich store of particles which in Greek served to express so precisely the logical relation of the clause; the circumstantiality and monotony of the expressions; and the fondness for antithesis and parallelism. Aramaic characteristics of speech are so predominant that some have been tempted to suppose an Aramaic original of the Greek text. The Gospel, which is relatively poor in direct quotations, is largely coloured by implicit references to the Hebrew Scriptures; and in the Epistle, which contains no direct quotations at all, the expression is so obviously moulded by the Old Testament that its Hebraistic affinity has been urged as a ground for distinguishing its author from that of the Gospel. In the same direction point the use of Hebrew words and names (rabbi, rabboni, Cephas, Messias, Gabbatha, Golgotha) especially the " verily verily " (amen amen), and the explanation of Siloam 9 7; the familiarity with the places and customs of Palestine, with the relations of Jews and Samaritans, and with the different parties within Judaism. These considerations justify us in seeking at least a close relation between S. John's thought and the theology of the Old Testament, and suggest the presumption that the *lacunæ* of his exposition are to be supplied from the current conceptions of contemporary Judaism.

The following construction of the Johannine theology proceeds from a recognition of these predominant characteristics of the author's thought: of the principle of contrast which is regulative of his thought through and through, and is expressed by Light and Darkness and the whole line of correlative antitheses; of the intuitive faculty which represents stages of development pictorially, dramatically, in terms of vision, rather than under the rubrics of logic; of the blending of subjective and objective, which without prejudice to the real importance of Christ's work represents, in a manner not exclusively yet characteristically Johannine, the accomplishment and content of salvation in terms of revelation, light, knowledge; and of the background of Jewish thought which determines the conception of God and of the world, and finds the specific content of salvation in a new and filial relation to God in the community of the chosen brotherhood. The great contrast is that between God and the world. This contrast is not so much resolved as revealed by the manifestation of the Logos, who even "in the flesh" is not a synthesis of God and not-God; but, as one who is essentially and perfectly God and Light he provokes in the Darkness a continual judgment ($κρίσις$) and separation between the light-loving elements and those which are constituted in their inmost nature children of the Devil. This manifestation of the Son of God in the world effects at once the destruction, " passing away," of the kingdom of evil and the gathering together of the children of God into one; and both are accomplished as well by what is objectively wrought by him, as by the inherent power of his revelation of the truth; — by his work as well as by his word.

This scheme of thought is presented under the following topics:

  I. God.
 II. The Logos with God.
III. The Kosmos lying in Darkness.
IV. The Life Manifested.
      A. Salvation out of the world.
          1. The doom of the world.
          2. Election of the children of God.
      B. Realisation of the positive concept of salvation.
          1. The New Birth.
          2. Eternal Life.
          3. The Children of God. — Fellowship.
             Likeness to God.
             Love.
             Confidence.
             Prayer.

THE THEOLOGY OF S. JOHN

I

GOD

GOD IS LIGHT

S. JOHN justifies the name of Theologian, which appears in the traditional title of the Apocalypse, **God the Centre of Theology** by the central position which he gives to the doctrine of God. Although the Gospel is professedly a history of Jesus' life, and the Epistle is mainly intent upon the solution of the practical problems of the Christian brotherhood, S. John's teaching is throughout and in the strictest sense *theology*. For the history which he records is in every detail the revelation of God, and his ethics is simply resolved into the imitation of God. There are advocates nowadays of a "Christo-centric" theology: the word is obviously a solecism; but nowhere is the impropriety of the distinction which is here raised between Christo-centric and Theo-centric better shown than in the writings of S. John. We have already remarked upon the absolutely central position which Christ occupies in S. John's thought; but we saw at the same time how in his Epistle he blends his reference to Christ with his reference to the Father. Christ is the centre of his theology, but just for that reason God is. For one of the prime articles of his faith is the profession of Christ "I and the Father are one" 10^{30}. The whole significance of Jesus depends upon his relation to God: upon the fact that as the only begotten Son he is the only "exegete" of the Father 1 18; as the Word (which in the beginning was with God, which *was God*) he was, not only in word, in work, in character, but in nature, the revelation of God. The high faith which he demanded in the last hour of intercourse with the disciples was, "*that I am in the Father and the Father in me; he that hath seen me hath seen the Father*" 14 9 10. And with all it is the Father and not the Son which is the centre of S. John's thought. The lofty self-consciousness of Jesus, which is so prominent in the Fourth Gospel, finds no higher expression than the relation of son to father; and precisely this Gospel which would teach the very highest significance of Jesus' Person is most untiring and emphatic in its assertion of the subordination of the Son as son. The assertion, "*The Father is greater than I*" 14 28, is not an anomaly, but the key-note of Jesus' self-witness. The passages are too numerous for reference in which Jesus himself testifies to the derivation of all his power from the Father. This is indeed implicit in the name itself, and is expressed in almost all of his utterances about the Father. It is the Father who sent him 12 49 6 39 8 16; his life and his death is in keeping with his Father's commandment 15 10 10 18; he came not to do his own but the Father's will 5 30; his works are the Father's works and done in his name 10 25 37; he speaks only of what he has seen 8 38, heard 15 15, and learnt 8 28 from the Father; his very *life* is derived from the Father 5 26 6 57; and his position in the world is completely characterised by this, that he is not as one who comes in his own name, but "I am come in my Father's name" 5 43.

It is clear from the foregoing that God is to S. John the subject of all-absorbing interest. And we are prepared for the solemn emphasis with which, in the opening of his Epistle 1 5, he sums up the good tidings of Christ in a single proposition about God: "*God is light, and in him is no darkness at all.*" There is in the whole range of the New Testament no second passage which can be placed along side of this as a considerate and solemn statement of the essential content of Christ's revelation to men. The importance which S. John attaches to this utterance is shown, not only by its immediate introduction, "*This is the message which we have received from him, and announce unto you*"; but by the position which it occupies at the beginning of the Epistle, and by the general introduction of the first four verses. These introductory verses make it plain that the message which he here summarises is not only what he had learnt from the words of Jesus, but is the epitome of his total manifestation. It is evident that S. John intends here to express, so far as language can express, "*the Word of life,*" "*the manifested life,*" "*what we have seen and handled,*" as well as "*what we have heard.*"

This passage is an important proof of the justness of S. John's judgment, the right proportion of his thought, which, with all its emphasis upon the saving revelation of Christ, realises that the message attains its highest and most universal expression, not in a proposition concerning the fate of man, but in a demonstration of the char-

Light

acter of God. That S. John was able to pack the Gospel message into one proposition, is due to the fact that he speaks in symbols; and precisely on this account is it difficult to give a matter of fact interpretation of this brief but all embracing definition. The employment of symbolical language is characteristic of S. John, and it is this which enables him to express his whole theology in the compass of a few profound ideas, the relations of which to each other undergo protean changes according as one or another side of the symbolical reference is predominant. This is an elusive mode of thought, and nowhere more so than in the case of the term light.

There is another respect in which this sentence is highly characteristic of S. John, namely in its antithetical form. It is in this case hardly more than a question of form, for the negative clause adds no new conception, though it gives definition, and heightens immensely the impression of moral conviction, with its impetuous denial: "*and darkness in him there is none!*"

The commonest use of the word light in S. John is also in accordance with the simplest and most obvious suggestion of the figure. When Jesus says "I am the light of the world" 8 ^{12} 9 $_5$, the term is apparently used with the same simplicity of significance as in Mat. 5 ^{14}, "Ye are the light of the world," denoting the pervading moral influence of pure example, Mat. 5 $^{13-16}$, it being the attribute of light that it shines and giveth light to all that are in the house, as it is of salt that it giveth savour to that with which it comes in contact. This simple application of the figure in the sense of moral revelation and enlightenment is still clearer in 12 35 36, "Yet a little while is the light among you. Walk while ye have the light, that the darkness overtake you not; and he that walketh in darkness knoweth not whither he goeth." But here the ethical meaning passes into the soteriological, "Believe on the light, that ye may become sons of light," and reminds us that with S. John the highest meaning which he attaches to a word is seldom quite absent from it, even in what appears a simpler and lower use. Nevertheless for the understanding of S. John's use of this term we must hold fast to the fact that its primary significance is that of revelation, manifestation. The most objective use of it in this sense is in 3 20 21, "For every one that doeth ill hateth the light, and cometh not to the light, lest his works should be reproved. But he that doeth the truth cometh to the light, that his works may be made manifest, that they have been wrought in God."

It must however be evident that this active signification falls short of many of S. John's uses of the term. And in fact the passage just quoted makes it clear how the terms light and darkness might acquire a purely ethical significance as the spheres, or even the very principles, of good and evil. In this sense S. Paul uses them, Eph. 5 8 9 6 12 II. Cor. 6 14, and that this is an element in S. John's idea is shown by his use of darkness in an active sense and as a positive concept I 5 12 35 I. 2 11. We can here observe the influence of the Old Testament point of view (common also in Greek generally), according to which light denotes a state of undisturbed happiness, of prosperity, and of salvation, just as darkness means a state of perdition, because every form and development of life is conditional upon light. In accordance with this, light with S. John denotes not only the condition of happiness 5 35, but of life itself 8 12. It hence gains a more positive content, as an effective force, a power which works a change in objects, as well as reveals their character. Still, all of this does not suffice to explain the use of the word in I. 1 5, where it is regarded, not as an active force, but as an immanent quality. *God is light* cannot be taken as an assertion of the essential nature of God as composed of light-substance, for this would be, to S. John especially, a matter of comparatively little interest, and could not in any sense be regarded as an expression — far less as the complete expression — of the revelation given in Christ. Neither can it denote merely the fact that God is a being clear and intelligible, and that self-revelation is his very nature; for the " walking in the light " and " in darkness " of the following verses dwells upon the ethical import of the terms. The fact is that S. John's use of light in this passage is so emphatic, so evidently considerate and weighty, that it is more reasonable to interpret all other uses of the term by means of this, than to narrow this magnificent statement to the dimensions of what is conceived to be his common use. Now it is absolutely certain that S. John found in Jesus the revelation of God as holiness, power, and love; and this much at least must be included in the expression *God is light*. And it is not hard to see how he came to use this expression in this sense. For regarding light primarily as revelation — that which reveals — and regarding Christ as *the* manifestation of the life I. 1 2 and of the truth, he could

not fail to think also of the content of the revelation,
— holiness, power, justice, love. For light is not
only that which reveals, it is also a substance of
particular character, and it is because of its substantial
character that it reveals, and not only reveals, but
"makes light" Eph. 5 13 whatever it manifests. It is
a beneficent power which produces joy and life. It
is therefore by no means strange that S. John should
employ this word to express the immanent quality of
God; nor does this expression stand alone, as is
commonly supposed; for we can read back from this
and see, in the sayings which describe Christ and the
Logos as light, the same conception, that he is the
sum of all the revelation of good which he brings.
And though the content of this saying must be
supplied from elsewhere, namely from the whole
Gospel, it is none the less a statement of the highest
importance. For it shows not only that God was the
essential subject of S. John's Gospel; but how absolutely the Logos — who was light — was conceived
as the revelation of God; — what the Logos manifested himself to be, that God is. And it shows how
thoroughly S. John grasped "the message" as good
tidings, as joy and life, as the brightest message that
could possibly be conceived; — "*no darkness at all.*"
Although this whole store of ideas is not *expressed* by
the term light itself, it was a matter of great moment
to S. John that he had a word with which he could
associate the whole sum of the Gospel message, and
the essential nature of God. It was characteristic
of S. John to express much in little, and we need not
be afraid to see in this word also an active signification.
As it is the very nature of the "word" to reveal, so

it is the nature of light to shine, to give light; and it is surely not going beyond S. John's idea, when we see here an expression of God's activity 5 17 towards his creatures; when we see, in the light which triumphs over the darkness, an expression of God's might; — a might which is especially manifested by the production of the fruits of light in the children who walk in his light I. 1 7. There is still another aspect under which God is thought of in relation to light. The divine Glory which from time to time was manifested to Israel was thought of as an envelope of light; and this idea has a marked influence upon the use of the word in the New Testament. We read: "the glory of God shone" Luke 2 9; "the brightness of his glory" Heb. 1 3; the light which overshadowed Christ on the mount is called "the glory" II. Pet. 1 17; and S. Paul in connection with the glory of Moses' countenance II. Cor. 3 7, speaks of "the light of the Gospel of the glory" 4 4, and "the light of the knowledge of the glory of God" 4 6. This idea is especially prominent in the Apocalypse: "the earth was lightened with his glory" 18 1, and "the glory of God did lighten it" 21 23. But in the writings which we are studying, the only passage in which it appears to have definitely influenced S. John's thought is I. 1 7 "as he is in the light." The form of this expression is doubtless determined by the parallel, "walk in the light," but it shows also how natural it was to speak of the light as the element in which God lives, as darkness is the element which characterises the world. There are obvious suggestions from many points of view for the choice of this symbol; but having once chosen it S. John invests it with a depth of meaning peculiarly his own, and the expression in I. 1 5 is so far from being a solitary use, that we must regard it rather as the climax of a series, and read back into even the apparently simple uses of the term something of the pregnancy of this extraordinary summary of theology, *God is light.*

THE TRUE GOD

The Logos become flesh revealed not only an *idea* of God characterised by attributes of goodness, mercy and love; but by revealing these qualities in his own person he reveals them as realities, and God as the essentially existing. S. John, like the other Apostolic writers, had no interest in the contention that God *is,* as the mere contradictory of the proposition God *is not;* but in a deeper sense, in the sense that God is the source of all existence, S. John does very strongly emphasise this proposition. He probably included this idea in his conception of light as the positive reality opposed to the negative darkness; but he had in the word *true* a less doubtful and more definite expression for it. The proposition "God is spirit" 4 24 includes not only the idea that his nature is different from the objects of sense; but more particularly and positively, that he is a *reality* of a higher sort. This is not a definition of merely speculative interest, its practical bearing is shown in the requisition that the true worshippers must worship God in "spirit and in truth" 4 23 24; — that is, in a way corresponding to reality. We shall see elsewhere how close is the relation of the words spirit and truth; and the relation also of the truth to faith and to salvation is discussed under another topic. Here we have to consider God as *the true* I. 5 20. This word, true, with the substantive and adverb, truth and truly, (ἀληθής, ἀληθινός, ἀλήθεια, ἀληθῶς, ἀμήν) are used so significantly by S. John that we have no need to rely upon the striking expression of the Apocalypse " Which is and which was and which is to come " I 4 8 to demonstrate his interest in the assertion of the essential reality of God's existence. The connection of Ex. 3 14 shows that the description of God as " the existing " (ὁ ὤν) is not prompted by a metaphysical interest, but in accordance with the practical character of Hebrew thought it is set forth as the ground of faith. So also the description of him as "the true" (τὸν ἀληθινόν) I. 5 20 is to be considered, according to the analogy of Hebrew thought, as the ground of the confidence of faith. The common connotation of the English words true and truth is, like the root meaning of the corresponding Greek words, a relative idea; it denotes the correspondence of an object with its idea, or, in an opposite sense, of an idea with the reality. On the other hand the root meaning of the Hebrew words (אמת, אמן) and their constant use, is similar to the root meaning of our English words and their occasional use. As true and truth are akin to troth and trust, so the whole range of words derived from the Hebrew root in question express faithfulness, reliability, and even faith itself. The Greek word has an intellectual cast, it has to do with ideas and their relation to the facts which they are assumed to represent; the Hebrew word deals primarily not with propositions, with their adequacy and veracity; but with persons and things, and it describes them as realities which may be leaned upon, relied upon, trusted. This range of Hebrew (Aramaic) words influences profoundly S. John's use of the corresponding Greek terms; the Hebrew meaning is super-added to the Greek, but as the word truth does not thereby lose its intellectual connotation, it is brought from this side also into close relation to faith as an act of perception. There is at least a striking commentary to this Hebraism of S. John's in Rev. 3 14. Christ is there called, by a simple transliteration of the Aramaic word, "the amen" ($\dot{a}\mu\acute{\eta}\nu$), and S. John merely translates this expression when he calls Christ or God "the true" ($\acute{o}$ $\dot{a}\lambda\eta\theta\iota\nu\acute{o}s$). The constant use of the double "amen amen" in S. John's Gospel is a sign of his attachment to this Hebrew word. There is a clear distinction in S. John's use of the two adjectives $\dot{a}\lambda\eta\theta\acute{\eta}s$ and $\dot{a}\lambda\eta\theta\iota\nu\acute{o}s$; the former abides more closely by the radical meaning of clear, manifest, that which is true in distinction from that which is mendacious, it remains a relative idea demanding another subject in regard to which the person or thing is true; it is $\dot{a}\lambda\eta\theta\iota\nu\acute{o}s$ which is used to express the positive, real rather than relative, significance of the Hebrew idea. It describes the subject in question in its absolute nature, and thereby ascribes to it truth as its proper and essential character. The contrast which defines $\dot{a}\lambda\eta\theta\acute{\eta}s$ is generally that between veracity and falsehood; while that suggested by $\dot{a}\lambda\eta\theta\iota\nu\acute{o}s$ is between essential and effective reality, and empty and deceptive appearance. The Hebrew analogy extends even to individual expressions. The connection of true and truth with witness 5 33 etc.

and with judgment 8 16 is thoroughly Hebraic. "He who sends me is true" 7 28 has its parallel in Jer. 26 15; "lead you into all the truth" 16 13, in Ps. 25 5. Truth and light 1 9 I. 2 8 are also brought into connection in the Psalter 43 3. The "true vine" 15 1 has its counterpart in Jer. 2 21. There are other instances in which the form of S. John's expression may be shown to be influenced by an Aramaic phrase, and still others in which his *idea* is seen to be thus determined.

After this general explanation we can approach the proper subject of this section with the consideration of the expression "full of grace and truth" in 1 14. The high significance which S. John attaches to this utterance is shown not only by the fact that it stands in the Prologue; but by the evident intention of summarizing in this verse the positive significance of Christ's manifestation; and by the contrast in which he sets this expression to the Old Testament revelation 1 17. It is significant too as the solitary recurrence in the New Testament of the Hebrew חסד ואמת ("lovingkindness and truth") so commonly applied to God's revelation of himself Ex. 34 6 II. Sam. 2 6 Ps. 25 10 40 10 11 86 15 98 3 115 1 138 2. This pair of ideas appears in the Synoptists in the form "mercy and faith" ($\tau\grave{o}$ ἔλεος καὶ ἡ πίστις) as qualities to be exercised by men; whereas S. John with "grace and truth" (ἡ χάρις καὶ ἡ ἀλήθεια) reproduces precisely the Hebrew idea of qualities displayed by God. In Ex. 34 6 the revelation of God is given in his solemn proclamation of his name as full of mercy and truth. When in the Prologue this solemn designation is transferred to the Logos, it is as an expression of his glory as the only begotten from the Father, and rests upon the fact that precisely as the only begotten Son he is the interpreter of the invisible God 1 18. The Law, which characterised the Old Testament economy 1 17, was but an imperfect revelation of God because it represented him only in terms of such injunctions as could be practically enforced in human society; whereas the more perfect revelation expressed by "the Name," which was in old time merely "proclaimed," was first "beheld" in the Word become flesh. That which was God's peculiar character and glory is at the same time Jesus' distinction, his personal possession and his gift to the world. Jesus himself is therefore *the truth* 14 6 because in him the sum of the qualities hidden in God is presented and revealed to the world. By the very fact of his coming in fulfilment of promise, by his coming in the flesh, and by the ethical quality of the life which he manifests, he reveals God as *the true*, in the sense of the faithful, the reliable, the absolutely real. The truth is divine; it does not come into being through human perception and speech, but exists in perfect completeness above and apart from any intellectual appreciation on the part of men. Only within the world can there be ascribed to it a becoming (ἐγένετο) 1 17, and here it acquires existence and might through Jesus' work and witness. The truth is divine, and yet S. John never speaks of God's truth, any more than of God's light, or of God's life. He does not distinguish a double light, human and divine; but light and life are a unit, belonging peculiarly to God, and what there is in the world of light and life is the product and gift of God. In the same way he concentrates the idea of truth into an undivided unity, it is God's nature and being, he is "the only true" (τὸν μόνον ἀληθινόν) 17 3. "The truth" does not comprise information upon every subject; it is limited to the revelation of God in Christ (or through the Spirit) 16 13-15. This which on one side expresses absolutely the divine nature as reality, expresses also its relation to men. For the truth has relation to the conscious spiritual activity of man, to the "understanding" (διάνοιαν), and can be "known" I. 5 8 32; "God's word is truth" 17 17; and so like "light" it represents God's nature in terms of an active force, and in relation to his rational creation. It is in this connection that the Spirit and the truth are brought into relation 4 23, the Spirit is "the Spirit of the truth" 14 17 15 26 16 13; "the Spirit is the truth" I. 5 6. In this connection too truth and life are brought together I. 5 20, and in their union constitute "the way" to God 14 6. All things in the world which have reality in the deepest sense partake of it from God; hence "the true light" 1 9 I. 2 8, "the true bread" 6 32, "the true food" and "drink" 6 55, "the true vine" 15 1. S. John speaks of that which is "truly love" I. 2 5 I. 3 18 in distinction from love which is mere pretence, of "the true worshippers" 4 23, of being "truly disciples" 8 31. The opposite of truth is a *lie*, a conception which does not merely indicate conscious and intentional deception; but the whole realm of mere appearance, of deception, of naught. As the truth belongs to God, so the lie characterises Satan, and he who in his inmost being is dependent on him and fashioned after him has him for "father." The truth, as God's nature, is the root of all worthy human existence; man may be "of the truth" 18 37 I. 3 19 as he may be "of God," and both conceptions coincide 18 37 8 47. The truth is connected both with knowledge and with deed; both expressions are used: "to know the truth," and "to do the truth" 8 32 3 21. In fact its closest relation is to deed, and only secondarily does it come into relation to knowledge 7 17 I. 1 6 3 18.

We have been obliged here to anticipate certain aspects of S. John's idea of truth which come more properly under another topic. It was necessary to study the word at once on all sides in order that we might understand the significance which S. John attached to the definition of God as the true. Under this term he describes him, not only as one who is veracious and faithful 3 33 (a covenant keeping God I. 1 9; — see faithful and true of the Apocalypse 3 14, also Holy and true, true and just); but as the essential reality. He describes him, not only as the true God in distinction from other national deities, and from "idols," but as " the alone true." We are in position now to appreciate the solemnity of the final utterance of the Epistle, in which S. John expresses the absolute confidence of his faith: "*And we know that the Son of God is come, and hath given us an understanding, that we know the True, and are in the True, in his Son Jesus Christ; — this is the true God and eternal life.*"

THE FATHER

That S. John thought of God very definitely as a person is a sure deduction from his relation to Hebrew thought; but it was also determined by the fact that God was revealed to him

Personality

in a person, Jesus. Therefore with all the use he makes of such abstract terms as light and truth, which are equally apt to describe an impersonal deity, and might represent his activity as readily in terms of emanation as of conscious voluntary action, his favourite name for God is "the Father."

S. John does not use the word, create ($\pi o\iota e\hat{\iota}\nu$); but ἐγένετο has practically that meaning in 1 3; and we might almost say that this verse — "without him," the Logos, "was not any thing made" — is expressly formulated to leave room for the superior creative activity of God. The close parallel, which we shall later study, between the Prologue and the first chapter of Genesis puts it beyond a doubt that S. John thought of God as Creator; the omission of a statement to this effect is merely significant of the fact that he did not dwell with any interest upon the material factors of the world.

The Creator

It was not however as Creator that God was Father. This much vaunted doctrine of "the Fatherhood of God" in the universal sense, is not a Christian idea at all; it has no point of contact with Hebrew thought, nor is there a single passage in the New Testament which expresses it; — except S. Paul's quotation before the Areopagus, from "certain of your poets": "For we are also his offspring." It is in fact a heathen idea, and is to be distinguished from the Christian idea, not only for the sake of historical accuracy, but because it is not capable of the depth of meaning which we find attached to God's Fatherhood in the New Testament and especially in S. John.

S. John, like the Greek poet, thinks of God's children as "his offspring" in a very real sense; not however *God the Begetter* in virtue of their material creation in the flesh, but of the new birth "*of the Spirit*" 3 3-7. S. John's expression in 1 12, "to them gave he the right to become children of God," suggests a nominal or legal conception of the status of the children of God, like S. Paul's sonship by adoption; but the real sense of fatherhood by begetting is expressed in the same sentence: "which were begotten, not of bloods, nor of the will of the flesh, nor of the will of man, but of God." And in I. 3 1 the privilege of merely nominal sonship is exceeded by the real relation: "Behold what manner of love the Father hath bestowed upon us, that we should be called children of God; — *and are*" (κληθῶμεν, καί ἐσμεν). This conception of the real nature of God's parental relation is everywhere predominant with S. John, and doubtless affected his choice of the word "children" (τέκνα) rather than sons (υἱοί), to express a likeness of nature rather than a position of privilege. The name *Son* is reserved for Christ.

The profound significance of S. John's idea of God, as the begetter of life, in relation to the children, *The only Begotten Son and the Children* is demonstrated by the fact that the same terms are used to describe his relation to the Son. The favourite expression which S. John uses to describe Christ's nature and privilege is that of "Son" 1 34 20 31 I. 2 22 23 5 5 20 etc.; and Jesus himself makes no higher claim 3 35 36 5 23 19 7. "The only begotten Son," an expression which S. John 1 14 I. 4 9 and Christ 3 16 18 both use, denotes his unique relation of love and privilege. Both terms suppose likeness, and Christ's fitness to reveal God rests upon the unique acquaintance of the only begotten Son with the Father and upon his likeness to him, I 18. Yet notwithstanding this peculiarity of his nature and position, notwithstanding also the fact that the children are never called sons (far less can any other be called *the* Son) there is a very close analogy between the position of the Son and of the children. The word *children* denotes privilege I 12, I. 3 1, and also likeness to God I. 3 2. Still more clearly does the act of *begetting* imply likeness in the children, as well as in the unique Son: "That which is born of the Spirit is spirit" 3 8; "If ye know that he is righteous, ye know that every one also that doeth righteousness is begotten of him" I. 2 29; "Every one that loveth is begotten of God" 4 7; in I. 3 9 it is expressly the "seed" of God which works conformity to his likeness, "Whosoever is begotten of God doeth no sin, because his seed abideth in him, and he cannot sin, because he is begotten of God." The analogy is brought out still more strongly in I. 5 1, where both are spoken of under the same term, "Whosoever believeth that Jesus is the Christ is begotten of God: and whosoever loveth him that begat loveth him also that is begotten of him," and in I. 5 18, "We know that whosoever is begotten ($\gamma\epsilon\gamma\epsilon\nu\nu\eta\mu\acute{\epsilon}\nu o\varsigma$) of God sinneth not; but that he that was begotten ($\gamma\epsilon\nu\nu\eta\theta\epsilon\acute{\iota}\varsigma$) of God," Jesus, "keepeth him."

This conception is founded in the idea of God as the source of all life, and is therefore intimately connected with S. John's idea of eternal life as the pre-eminent gift of God in Christ. That God is life, is with S. John — although it is not expressed in the same way — an idea co-ordinate with, "God is love," "God is light," and "the true God." The idea of the divine Fatherhood is compounded of the two ideas, life and love: the true God is also eternal life I. 5 20. We have to note again that in connection with God's Fatherhood S. John is not thinking of life in the earthly sense, but always in the profound significance which he attaches to eternal life. In this sense God alone is the source of life, "the Father has life in himself, and to the Son he gave to have life in himself" 5 26. Thus the Son becomes the medium of life for men 1 · 6 57, and he it is in a sense who constitutes them the children of God 1 12. Christ is therefore himself "the life" 11 25 14 6; he is "the bread of life" 6 35; and apart from him there is no life possible for men I. 5 11 12.

God the Source of Life

The idea of the new birth is not peculiar to S. John (compare παλινγενεσίας Tit. 3 5 and ἀναγεννήσας I. Peter 1 3 23); but the connection of this idea with that of the divine Fatherhood, the welding of three several ideas into one chain — the Father, begetting, life — is altogether his own. When we come however to consider the ethical relation involved in fatherhood, it is not at first so obvious in what respect S. John has exceeded even the Jewish standpoint. It is true that in the Old Testament Scriptures it was only the rarer heights of psalmody and prophecy which rose to the conception of God as a Father; it had not become a current name. In contemporary Judaism however, as the New Testament itself is sufficient to prove, it had already become a familiar designation of God, a

The Father of the Nation

common address in prayer, and a boast of Jewish privilege. There is in the Synoptic account no hint that Christ's common reference to "your Father" was in any way strange to Jewish ears. On the other hand the expression "my Father" gave the highest offence, according to John 5 ¹⁸; and evidently because God was regarded as the Father of the covenant Nation as a whole, and so while the common address " Our Father" 8 ⁴¹ was in vogue the particular claim was disallowed. In the Synoptic accounts it seems as if Christ were constantly bent upon bringing home to his disciples the Father's individual relationship to them and care for them. This same purpose is accomplished also according to S. John's narrative, but in a widely different way. S. John, so far from particularising the relationship, seems to generalise it; his phrase is "the Father," never "our Father," and but once "your Father." This phrase however does not denote a fatherhood of wider range; it is not the Father and mankind, but "*the Father and the Son*," "the Father" equals "my Father." In S. John's Epistle particularly "the Father" appears as a set theological designation of God in distinction from "the Son," and the name is used with the same significance even in the speeches of Christ in the Gospel. That it was so used by Christ is by no means impossible (it was not a late theological development, it is not only the terminology of S. Paul, but of the strictly Jewish-Christian circle, Acts 2 ₃₃ Jas. 1 ²⁷ 3 ⁹); but it is impossible to suppose that he confined himself to this strict use, that he did not commonly use also the familiar Synoptic phrases "your Father" and "our Father."

S. John's own peculiar mode of representation is, however, excellently designed to display Christ's method of bringing home to his disciples the intimacy of God's relation as Father. Just as the significance of the Father as the begetter of life is seen primarily in his relation to the only begotten Son; so too the Father's ethical relation to the children is interpreted in terms of his loving relation to the Son. The constant representation of S. John's Gospel is to the effect that Jesus did not speak in the terms of popular usage of the Fatherhood of God as a relation common to himself and his disciples; but that he appropriated it peculiarly to himself, and thereby immeasurably exalted the intimacy and the reality of the conception. When he speaks of the Father it is almost always in relation to himself and in a way which is practically equivalent to my Father. He emphasises his unique knowledge of the Father 6 46 (compare Luke 10 22), and the Father's unique love toward him 3 35 5 20 17 24. This relationship is so close that he can say "I and the Father are one" 10 30, "I am in the Father and the Father in me" 14 11, and he is in such sense the medium between the Father and the children, that God's love to men is conditioned by their love to Christ 14 20-23.

The Father and the Son

The significance of this strictly consistent usage of S. John lies in this, that having so deepened the idea of the Father as the most intimate and personal relationship of love, he all at once in his last hour of communion with his own transfers to them the fulness of this divine paternity, in the saying: *"My Father and your Father"* 20 17.

The Father and the Children

In his high-priestly prayer he says, "that the love wherewith thou lovest me may be in them" 17 26. Having brought his disciples into this relationship of children to the Father, he has brought them so close, he has established a relationship so real, that his own mediatorial position is in a sense superseded; for though the disciples are instructed to pray in his name 16 24, he nevertheless adds, "I say not unto you that I will pray the Father for you; for the Father himself loveth you" 16 26 27. Though our union with the Father is mediated by the Son, ("I in them and thou in me" 17 23 14 20) it is not on that account less real and close; for S. John speaks in his Epistle of "our fellowship with the Father and with his Son Jesus Christ" I 3 as co-ordinate relations. We "abide in the Son and in the Father" I. 2 24, for with S. John the one includes the other, and we see again the significance of his loose employment of the personal pronouns, when he says, "hereby know we that we are in him" I. 2 5. The Father has displayed his active interest by the fact that he "hath sent the Son, the Saviour of the world" I. 4 14; and he it is who also sends the Spirit of truth as "another Comforter" 14 16 26 who like Christ abides in us 14 17.

It is very clear that the more richly the idea of God's Fatherhood is developed, so much the more impossible is it to think of it in relation to the world in general. At any rate in S. John's doctrine of the Father, as defined by the whole range of ideas with which it is associated, the relation is limited to those whom Christ has chosen out of the world 15 19. It is evident that the chain of ideas which with S. John constitute one side of the divine Fatherhood (the particular act of begetting, the new birth, and eternal life) were not realised in the case of all men. Even "his own" (the nation which boasted that God was their Father 8 41) received Christ not 1 11, thereby proving that they were not true children of God 8 42; "but as many as received him, to them gave he the right to become children of God" 1 12. God's Fatherhood therefore is no longer limited to the Nation; his children are scattered abroad and are brought together into one community by Christ's death 11 52.

S. John is not unjustly lauded as the Apostle of love. A strong emphasis upon love is common to the New Testament writers, but S. John is more than all others insistent upon it, both as an attribute of God and as the duty of man. God's love is an attribute of his Fatherhood, and in this deeper sense its sphere is of course limited to the children: "Behold what manner of love the Father hath bestowed upon us, that we should be called children of God" **God is Love** I. 3 1; "Herein was the love of God manifested in our case, that God hath sent his only begotten Son into the world, that we might live through him" I. 4 9. From this last verse we see too that God was revealed as love, not only by Christ's loving service and sacrifice I. 3 16; but by the very sending of the only begotten Son as a veritable sacrifice on the part of the Father; and that his love is thereby revealed not as a complacent affection, but as an active impulse.

We must notice here, as we shall have to do again, that notwithstanding S. John's representation of the children as chosen out of the world, and of the world itself as wholly evil, wholly opposed to God; he nevertheless regards God's love and his purpose of salvation in a universal aspect. God's relation to men as Creator is wider than that as Father, and as Creator too he loves his creatures. God's love moreover is not in the last resort founded upon man's love to him: "Herein is love, not that we loved God, but that he loved us, and sent his Son to be the propitiation for our sins" I. 4 ^{10} ^{19}. "God so loved the world, that he gave his only begotten Son, that whosoever believeth on him should not perish, but have eternal life" 3 ^{16}. In this verse we have the most universal expression of God's love towards his whole rational creation. This love of God, not only towards the Son, and the children, but towards his whole universe, is after all the necessary deduction from the principle that in his very nature, and independent of object, *God is love* I. 4 $_9$ $_{16}$.

II

THE LOGOS WITH GOD

JESUS' SELF-WITNESS

WE have seen in the last chapter that the love of God (which is not an occasional manifestation of his will, but the constant and essential attribute of his nature) was, in the broadest sense, directed toward the world; more particularly, toward the children chosen out of the world; and in a unique sense, toward the only begotten Son. We have to observe now that God's love was never without an object; but that even "before the world was," "in the beginning," God had in the Son the most perfect object and the most complete reciprocation of his love. This is included in Jesus' self-witness, according to S. John, and constitutes one of the most notable traits of the Fourth Gospel. Upon the predominance of Jesus' self-witness in the Fourth Gospel, and upon its relation to the aim of the author, we have already commented (pages 25–27). We have here to study the precise content of his claim in so far as concerns his relation to God. Jesus' *own* witness is expressed in terms of Sonship: *S. John's* doctrine of Jesus' Person is most characteristically formulated in connection with the term Logos. With all that we have already observed of S. John's assimilation of Jesus' speeches to the peculiarities of his own diction,

The Only Begotten Son

it is notable in this instance to what extent he distinguishes the form and content of Jesus' self-witness from his own dogmatic deductions. Not only does he never attribute the use of the term Logos to Jesus; but in his own pronouncements in the Prologue and in the Epistle he associates both with the Logos and with the Son ideas which advance beyond the explicit terms of Jesus' self-witness. The distinction is so clear that some even base upon it the claim of a difference of authorship as between the Prologue and the rest of the Gospel. It is however only by minimising the significance of Jesus' claim to be the Son of God, and by extravagantly embellishing S. John's doctrine of the Logos, that any incongruity can be proved. The fact is rather calculated to enhance our estimation of the historicity of the account; for it shows that the author was conscious of a distinction between what he had learned directly from the teaching of Jesus and what he had gained through meditation upon the things which he had seen and heard, and that he was not disposed to obscure that distinction in any essential part of his representation.

The inquiry as to the meaning of the expression "the Son of God" is commonly embarrassed by the prepossession that it must have but one definite significance. The fact is rather that with S. John it must, almost as a matter of course, be susceptible of many meanings. Here too we have to deal with a term which was of cardinal importance in Jesus' own teaching; and we might reasonably expect to find his pædagogical method illustrated here as it is elsewhere by the use of a term capable of ascending significance. Jesus adopted the name, kingdom of

God, not because in its familiar connotation it actually conveyed to the people his idea, but because it was *capable* of expressing it. The confession that Jesus is the Christ meant one thing in the early days of his ministry, and doubtless quite another and higher thing after his resurrection. He was accustomed, as a method of teaching, to seize upon an expression which was current in a lower significance, and raise it to its highest terms. This pædagogical principle is peculiarly clear in the use of the word Son; for it was more obviously a matter of choice, not forced upon him as a necessary element of the current Messianic terminology; and in the second place, not being an arbitrary expression but a natural analogy, it was peculiarly apt for the purpose of raising the disciples from a lower, through a whole range of ascending significations, to the highest conception. We have already seen how Jesus enhanced and enriched the word Father; we have an exact parallel in his use of the word Son. S. John was prompt to appreciate a method of teaching which was so thoroughly in harmony with his own type of thought; and, although it is sometimes asserted that he does not note as the Synoptists do a progression in the self-witness of Jesus, it is rather true, if we attend to this peculiarity, that he marks more clearly than others the progress of the disciples' appreciation of the significance of Jesus' claim. There is, corresponding to the progress of Jesus' ministry, a certain advance in the nature and clearness of his claim; and though this is less formally marked in the Fourth Gospel than elsewhere, it is the Fourth Gospel pre-eminently which furnishes the clue to the progress and culmination of the Messianic controversy to which Jesus' appearance gave rise; — which reveals at each stage the new estimation (on the part of those who reject him as well as of those who receive) of Jesus' claim, which in itself remains constant in the assertion of his divine Sonship. The expression "Son of God" is therefore with S. John not a constant quantity, but an ascending scale, it runs through the whole gamut, from the expression of a relation which every Israelite might claim 10 35 36, (Ps. 82 6), up to the definite note of divinity I. 5 20 21. From this point of view there is really no difficulty in understanding S. John's use of this term; for there is no longer any necessity of paring down the highest and most definite expressions to match the simplest use.

We shall find that the notion of Christ's Sonship gains a special significance from its connection with the peculiar elements of Johannine thought, but in the name itself there is of course nothing peculiar to S. John. It is used also by the Synoptists, but with this difference, that whereas in the Fourth Gospel it represents Christ's constant claim from the beginning, in the Synoptic Gospels it appears as the witness which the most striking aspects of his manifestation extort from his disciples, and as the culmination of his self-witness in the very end of his ministry. With the Synoptists "the Son of man" is the predominating expression, and serves as a transition to the higher name; with S. John the expression "the Son of God" is, as we have seen, itself capable of effecting the transition from lower to higher, and "the Son of man" though used in much the same way has its own peculiar significance more distinctly marked. The absolute expression "the Son" is common to both, though it is much more frequent in S. John. It occurs in fact but once (exclusive of its use in the parables) in the Synoptic account Mat. 11 27 (Luke 10 22): *All things have been delivered unto me of my Father: and no one knoweth the Son, save the Father; neither doth any know the Father, save the Son, and he to whomsoever the Son willeth to reveal him.* This single utterance however corresponds so precisely in form and substance to the more frequent expressions concerning the Son and the Father in the Fourth Gospel 6 46 10 15 that we cannot fail to see in it a hint of a more common use of "the Son of God" and "the Son" than the Synoptists have expressly recorded.

It was probably an advantage of the term, Son of God, that it had no such current use in the Old Testament as would definitely fix its meaning.

Divinity of the Son

It is applied to the Children of Israel as the highest expression of their relation to God, and more particularly to Israel's theocratic king. It is doubtless in no higher sense that, in the Book of Enoch and in the Fourth Book of Esdras, God is represented as calling the Messiah his Son. We have besides this no other information except that derived from the New Testament concerning the relation of this term to the Messianic idea. From the Gospels we gather that the term was actually associated with the Messianic hope, and that Jesus could not call himself the Son of God without suggesting a Messianic claim. We see however that the emphasis with which he employed the name suggested a significance much higher than was popularly accorded to the Messiah 10 33. The Old Testament uses the term "begotten" as a metaphor in connection with the divine Sonship Ps. 2 7; but we have already seen that S. John uses the idea of begetting in a real sense, as an analogy, even in connection with the Children of God, and we might expect that as the Father's love was shown in an altogether unique way towards *the* Son, so the idea of begetting in reference to him would have a value absolutely *sui generis*. The expression "only begotten Son," which is peculiar to S. John, represents primarily the relation of tender love; but it can hardly fail to have also with S. John the significance of real derivation from the divine nature I. 5 1. The children also were begotten; but if the relation of the Son to the Father were upon the same plane as that of the children, we should expect him to be called, as by S. Paul, "the first begotten among many brethren" Rom. 8 29 — see Rev. 1 5. Instead of that he occupies an absolutely singular relation to God as the *only* begotten Son. S. John still further heightens the distinction of Christ's position by refraining from the use of the expression sons (υἱοί) of God in relation to men, and by substituting for it the word children (τέκνα). It must be affirmed that the ethical relation which is everywhere prominent in the expression which we are studying rather suggests than excludes a substantial relation. There is no doubt that in the Epistles "the Son" denotes a nature more closely allied to God than to man. The constant conjunction of the Son and the Father is of itself sufficient to establish S. John's doctrine on this subject. It may even be asserted that there is nothing in S. John's Epistle to suggest any discrepancy between his employment of the names Father and Son, and their significance in the Trinitarian formula. The believer's relation to the Father and to the Son is expressed in the same terms I. 2 ²²⁻²⁴, and the last verse but one of the Epistle includes both " him that is true, and his Son Jesus Christ" in the affirmation, "This is the true God and everlasting life." There is also no doubt that "the only begotten Son" of the Prologue is substantially equivalent to "the Logos," and it therefore makes no difference whether verse 14 is to be translated "as an only begotten," or "as the only begotten;"—in either case he shares the divine "glory." Jesus' self-witness can hardly be said to fall short of this, though it may perhaps be more justly said to lead up to it. He too calls himself the only begotten Son 3 ¹⁶ ¹⁸; he is *the* Son, and he uses this name in the same significant association with the Father as it is used in the Epistle. When he said " my Father worketh even until now, and I work," he so associated himself with the Father as to justify the claim of the Jews that in calling "God his own Father" he was "making himself equal with God" 5 ¹⁷ ¹⁸. In 8 ⁵⁴ he discriminates his own position very sharply from that of the Jews in the contrast " my Father—your God." Again Christ's claim to be Son of God was accounted by the Jews to be equivalent to, " That thou being a man, makest thyself God"; and although Jesus shows how a lower meaning might be attached to the term Son of God, it cannot be supposed to be S. John's intention to represent him as disclaiming the higher significance

10 33-36. Still again, before Pilate, it is charged against him as the sin of blasphemy that he "made himself the Son of God" 19 17. This identification with God, though it was not necessarily included in the name Son, was plainly enough expressed in Jesus' self-witness. What the Father doeth, that doeth the Son; as the Father quickeneth, so the Son quickeneth whom he will; like the Father, the Son also has life in himself; and men must honour the Son even as they honour the Father 5 19-26. He claims that "all things which the Father hath are mine" 16 15; "He that hath seen me hath seen the Father" 14 19; he says "Believe in God, believe also in me" 14 1; he demands for himself the same sort of belief, "that I am" 8 24; he identifies himself with the Father in a very remarkable way when he says, "*we* will come unto him and make our abode with him" 14 23. It is in the light of such testimony we must read the claim, "I and the Father are one" 10 30, and "I am in the Father and the Father in me" 14 11; and not reduce it to the dimensions of the similar expressions which denote the relation of believers to God.

When on the other hand Jesus says, "My Father is greater than I" 14 28; when he represents his powers 5 26 36, his doctrine 8 28, and his mission 4 34 5 as derived from the Father; there is nothing to hint at any difference other than that which is assumed in the relation of Sonship and Fatherhood.

Jesus' self-witness was given like God's revelation of old time in divers portions and in divers manners. He did not straightway announce his highest claims; he strove to lead men up to the loftiest appreciation of his person. He did not even at the end sum up the divers elements of his self-witness in a single adequate statement; for even at the end he had many things to say to the disciples which they could not bear till after the resurrection. In particular he did not make the express claim that he was God; he doubtless could not have done so without thereby putting a fatal stumbling-block in the way of the disciples' growing faith 20 [28]. But if we sum up the details of Jesus' testimony about himself, without the least sophistication of exegesis, the total impression can hardly be other than this: that he had the consciousness and made the claim of being of the same nature as God. If we cannot suppose that S. John appreciated the metaphysical analysis which is presupposed in the expression "the same substance" in the Nicene Creed, we can surely express his conception of Jesus' witness, by saying that he in contrast with men was of the same *kind* as God.

Still another question arises, whether Jesus expressed the fact of his pre-existence, or left it to **Pre-existence** be inferred from his general claim of **of the Son** divinity. The fact is however that Jesus' consciousness of pre-existence is so clearly expressed in the Fourth Gospel that one wonders how it can be called in question. It is not proved by the frequent expressions which represent him as "sent" or even "sent into the world;" for such expressions are used of John the Baptist and others. Nor is it indubitably expressed in the claim of learning from the Father, of doing and saying what he has seen and heard with him; for this might conceivably be the result of inspiration and of inspired vision. There are other expressions too which denote derivation from God, but not pre-existence:—"I came forth and am come from God" S *cf.* 17 8. We might certainly rely with great confidence upon the many expressions which represent him as coming down from heaven 3 31 6 33 38 41 42 51; but this is still further defined by statements which would seem to admit of no possibility of misunderstanding. He speaks of "the Son of man ascending where he was before" 6 62; he says "I came out from the Father, and am come into the world; again I leave the world, and go unto the Father" 16 28. In his great prayer he says, "for thou lovedst me before the foundation of the world" 17 24; and he speaks of "the glory which I had with thee before the world was" 17 5. In the light of this clear witness, we can read the significance even of those statements which we have but just now set aside as insufficient *of themselves* to denote Christ's heavenly origin. But Jesus' testimony does not end here, with the claim of relative pre-existence. He demands belief in himself as the absolute existence: "Believe that I *am*" 8 24; "Before Abraham was I *am*" 8 59. It is impossible to interpret this strange saying, without connecting it (cf. Rev. 1 4 etc.) with the solemn proclamation of God's name I AM recorded in Ex. 3 14. In this reference we see the full significance of Jesus' claim.

S. JOHN'S DOCTRINE OF THE LOGOS

The foregoing discussion has been limited to the proof of two propositions: that the self-witness of Jesus in the Fourth Gospel expresses a consciousness of pre-existence, and leads up to the statement of his

S. John's Own Estimate of Christ

divinity 20 ²⁸. It has thereby omitted very many items of Jesus' claim, some even which are germane to the topic and others which are more properly discussed in relation to his Messianic mission in the world. So predominant is Jesus' self-witness in the Fourth Gospel, and so rich is its content, that a full and detailed discussion of it is incompatible with either the brevity or clearness of the exposition we have in hand. Most of Jesus' utterances, and most of the pragmatic situations of the Gospel, bear on this point; for it was in this interest (pp. 26 *seq.*) that the Gospel was composed.

That which S. John represents as Jesus' express teaching cannot however be studied apart from his own estimation of Jesus' Person. We see even in the Fourth Gospel how S. John, like the rest of the Apostles, beginning with the Baptist's witness to the Lamb of God 1 ³⁶, quickly rose from the mere respect due to Jesus as *Rabbi* 1 ³⁸ to an appreciation of him as *the Messiah* 1 ⁴¹. But S. John's Gospel is not so well designed to display the origination and development of his faith, as it is to express his ultimate conclusion. And although the confession, that Jesus is the Christ, was doubtless raised to a much higher significance than he at first accorded it; although it is included in his statement of the aim of his Gospel ("That ye might believe that Jesus is the Christ, the Son of God" 20 ³¹), and remains to the last the orthodox confession of faith; the name itself was not capable of expressing S. John's highest conception of what Jesus was in himself and in his relation to God. The name Son of God on the other hand, as we saw incidentally under the preceding topic, proved itself adequate at every stage for the expression of the new meaning with which it was associated. We have seen also that there is a difference to be noted between the self-witness of Jesus according to the Fourth Gospel and S. John's own utterances about him; though the trend of the foregoing discussion has been to show how slight after all the difference is. The historical manifestation of Jesus as interpreted by his self-witness in word and work was not only the foundation and starting-point of S. John's belief, but in the main covers it, and coincides with it, even in the form of expression. Beyond this however S. John does advance; and by sinking himself deeper and deeper in the contemplation of the eternal divine existence of the Son he reaches a standpoint which was possible only in the light of Christ's resurrection, and which he is scrupulous to distinguish, in some respects at least, from Jesus' own testimony. This developed point of view he presents not at the end of his Gospel, like S. Thomas' confession "*My Lord and my God*," which was the culminating expression of the disciples' faith after the Resurrection; but at the very beginning, and as the standpoint from which the whole earthly history of Christ must be regarded.

This advance which S. John makes beyond the express testimony of Christ, and this manner of treating history, are commonly described as speculative. This word, although we cannot strictly refuse to admit it, suggests almost inevitably an erroneous idea of S. John's method. S. John's speculation (pp. 38 *seq*.), if it may be so called, is at all events not of the dialectical sort which advances by a

<small>S. John's Use of the Term Logos</small>

chain of reasoning from one proposition to another; it does not start with an *a priori* thesis (as it is assumed to do in the so-called doctrine of the Logos) and work out a rational system: but it starts with given fact which it is intent upon understanding in its relations and in its deepest nature. S. John is interested not in pursuing deductions from, but in seizing and expressing the very nature of, the object of his contemplation; and hence it is that a name becomes not his starting-point, but his goal. A name has with S. John the same deep significance which is accorded it in all Semitic thought. It is not a fulcrum for argument, a premise suggesting further conclusions; but a finished product, a minted coin, the significance of which lies in the fact that it already perfectly expresses the nature of the object which it names. It is precisely this value that the name Word has for S. John, and the degree of importance which he attached to it is to be seen not so much in the Prologue and in the Epistle, as in Rev. 19 [13] "*His name is called the Word of God*" (cf. verse 12). Nothing could be more unreasonable than the assertion that Philo's philosophy of the Logos furnished S. John with an entirely new conception of Christianity. His sober and restrained use of the term is of itself enough to refute such a claim. It is a pure assumption which on the mere pretext of this name foists upon S. John a cosmological philosophy of emanations which is not borne out by any of the affirmations which he actually makes about the Logos. Neither can it be proved that his use of this name has any point of contact with the contemporary rabbinical personification of the Word and Wisdom, which seems also to be a product of the current philosophy of emanations. It remains at the most a possibility that the name Logos was familiar in some such sense to S. John and to the circle for whom he wrote, and that his adoption of it was thereby suggested and facilitated. But the actual content of his idea is drawn exclusively from the Old Testament; and inasmuch as this is an adequate explanation of the origin of the term, any other is superfluous. Moreover S. John's doctrine of the Word is wrought out so characteristically, and correlated so closely with his ideas of light and life, as to suggest that, even if we were to consider it a highly speculative system, we must consider it a system original with S. John.

The truth is, the common opinion to the contrary notwithstanding, that S. John's idea of the Logos is not a thing deeply mysterious and unintelligible; but one which, both in its origin and meaning, The Motive of S. John's Choice of the Term Logos is quite peculiarly clear. Neither is it in any wise the key, but the incidental product of his system of thought. This being the case we shall see more clearly as we advance in the study of S. John how precisely this word was adapted to his thought. But we have already seen enough of the general characteristics of his thought to enable us to appreciate at this point the motive of his choice.

We are puzzled at first to account for the necessity for any name higher than that of Son to express Jesus' divine nature and relationship. We have studied the exalted significance which S. John attaches to this name. His affirmation in regard to the Son rises to a supreme height when at the conclusion of the Epistle he says, "This is the True God and everlasting Life." Still more significant would be the assertion of 1.18, if we may accept a strongly supported text — "the only begotten *God*." This expression retains the idea of begetting which is implied in sonship (including the ideas of origin, of love and of dutiful subordination), and at the same time affirms absolute identity of nature. Such an expression cannot be accounted unnatural to S. John; but it is obviously ill adapted to the solution of the problem which confronted him, and for which he was seeking not so much an explanation as a name. The name Son indeed so far from solving rather throws into relief the problem which for S. John and the Church of his age was substantially the same as that which engaged the Church during the three succeeding centuries; and which in both instances was solved in much the same way. The problem was this: that having risen to an appreciation of the Son, as not only in a general sense divine, but of the same kind as God, and actually God; and yet at the same time (as was inevitable from the whole character of Jesus' manifestation and self-witness) personally distinguished from God; his belief seemed to be set in irreconcilable contradiction to the fundamental monotheism ingrained in his race. This contradiction could not fail to be felt so soon as his faith emerged from the purely practical sphere into the light of reasoned thought. The problem expressed itself in the form of an equation: The Father who is God *plus* the Son who is God = one God. To a Hebrew who believed that Jesus was God in a real sense this was the problem of problems; — incomparably more pressing than that of God's relation to the world. And this was the problem which S. John met by the use of the name Logos. The name Son was unsuited to meet this precise difficulty, because its chief stress lay upon the idea of personality, and so upon the distinction in the Godhead. What was wanted was a name which would designate Jesus according to his nature, and in substantial identification, not only with God in the abstract, but with the God of the Old Testament. We can state thus precisely the problem to be solved; but we cannot by any means affirm that S. John could have solved it in only one way; nor can we presume to point out the steps which necessitated his choice of the name Logos; — or in fact of any solution at all. We can see however how the choice was materially narrowed by certain important considerations. For if it is actually the Apostle John with whom we have to deal, nothing is more sure than that he must seek his solution, not in the metaphysical conceptions of Greek thought, but in the more naïve forms of Semitic (particularly Old Testament) representation. In the second place, S. John's predominant interpretation of salvation in terms of revelation (the Life of God becoming the light of men, and producing life in them) suggests at least that this thought must be made prominent also in his chosen designation for Christ. This we actually see realized in the choice of the term Logos or Word, which was suggested, not by the poetical personification of the Old Testament, but by its simplest and most ordinary employment in the formula of prophecy (" The word of the Lord came to me,") and in the creative fiat (" And he said — and it was so "); — as the word of power, and as the word of revelation.

The study of the first three verses of the Epistle serves at once to justify the foregoing argument, and to introduce us to the essential content of S. John's idea of the Logos.

Content of the Doctrine of the Logos

1. "*That which was from the beginning, that which we have heard, that which we have seen with our eyes, that which we beheld and our hands handled, concerning the Word of life* 2. (*and the life was manifested, and we have seen, and bear witness, and declare unto you the life, the eternal, which was with the Father, and was manifested unto us*); 3. *that which we have seen and heard declare we unto you also, that ye also may have fellowship with us.*"

It is a matter of discussion in the first place whether "the Word of life" in this passage is used in the same personal significance which it has in the Prologue, or merely in the sense of the life-giving revelation which Christ brought. This question is at least serious enough to suggest how very readily this expression might rise from the designation of Christ's saving revelation to the name for the Revealer himself. According to the common New Testament use, "the word of God," "the word of the Lord," or simply "the word," denotes the powerful, life-giving revelation of the Gospel, Heb. 4 12; it is not applied to the Old Testament as a whole, but only to such sayings as contain a prophecy of the Gospel, or are actually the expression of God's own message to the prophets. With S. John especially all the words of Christ are a powerfully energetic revelation; all Christ's sayings are thought of as an unit I. 2 5 etc.; this word is to be kept, for it is itself a commandment I. 2 7; it is the truth, and as such directly sanctifies 17 17; its reception delivers from death 8 51 and from judgment 12 47; the words ($ῥήματα$) of Christ are spirit and life 6 63. In the Apocalypse also "the word of God" is used with very marked emphasis, even where it is not, as in 19 13, employed as a personal name. When we note how closely "the Word of life" I. 1 1 seems to be related to this usage, we can realize how natural after all was S. John's use of the name Word in the Prologue. But even in this verse we cannot admit that the expression means simply the revelation of life; — if for no other reason, because it would leave us without any clew to explain the extraordinary grammatical construction, and in particular the change from the relative construction to the prepositional phrase "*concerning* ($περί$) the Word of life." The verb of the whole sentence is "we declare" ($ἀπαγγέλ-λομεν$), and if it was simply a question of the message which he had heard from Christ S. John must inevitably have construed it as the direct object of the verb, as in verse 5. It is obvious too that the content of this clause is defined by the relative clauses which precede it: "That which was from the beginning, which we have heard, seen, handled, etc." What does S. John intend by that? He surely does not mean the Son of God himself; or why should he express himself so strangely in the neuter? Moreover we should in this case have in I. 1 1 something different presented as the object of his declaration from that which is named in I. 1 2. Substantially at least the content of the first verse must be the same as that eternal life which, in the second, is declared to have been with the Father and to have been manifested unto us; — only in form it is not then thought of as the concrete representation of eternal life, but, abstractly, as that which constituted the eternal nature of the Son, and yet was revealed in sensible, historical manifestation. The Son of God was the subject of the saving message of the Gospel precisely in so far as in him was, and was manifested, that true and eternal life which being manifested became light I 4 — that is, the revelation of the true God and of his Son Jesus Christ — and so by bringing to men the knowledge of God, mediated to them the eternal life itself I7 3. It is this essential nature of the Son of God which the Apostle would represent as the content of his declaration; and in order to embrace this in one word, he breaks the relative construction with this clause, "concerning the Word of life"; — the Word himself was not the subject of his declaration, but that which had been manifested as his essential nature. When in I. 1 5 he sums up the message in the declaration, "God is light," this is indeed the summary of Jesus' manifestation in word and work, but it is not the Logos himself; — therefore the expression, "concerning the Logos." The controversy is idle, whether "the Word of life" represents the Word which has life, or the Word which gives life; for we have already seen that according to S. John's most characteristic mode of thought he is both. The essential nature of the Son of God is marked not only by the fact that he has eternal life in himself, but that he is able to impart it to men. Therefore it is that in the relative clause the fact of his existence in the beginning is associated with his historical manifestation; and the life is spoken of as that "which was with the Father and was manifested unto us."

We see, therefore, from the first verses of the Epistle that the term "Word," though it is strictly a personal title of Christ, designates him not so much according to his personality, as according to his essential nature; and this accounts for a mode of expression which is often held to suggest that "the Word of life" is here used quite impersonally and as a designation of the Gospel revelation. When we turn to the Prologue we find the term Word employed in quite the same way, but with more various and more express associations. It is there stated that "the Word was in the beginning." The expression of the first verse of the Epistle — "from the beginning" — is slightly different, because the Word is there considered only in so far as he is the subject of the Gospel proclamation, that is, as he was historically manifested to the senses; whereas in the Prologue we are pointed to his timeless existence "with God." It was similarly stated in the second verse of the Epistle that "the life was *with* the Father," and it is justly remarked that the preposition πρός instead of παρά denotes not mere juxtaposition, but lively personal community. A stricter, though unidiomatic, rendering would be "*towards* God." It is further stated, and by a turn of expression which is very emphatic, that "the Logos *was God.*" This triple affirmation is in a certain degree isolated from, not to say contrasted with, the statements which follow. It constitutes the complete expression of what the Word is in his relation to God. In verses 2 and 3 it is announced that he who was in the beginning with God became the medium of creation: "All things were made through him, and without him was not anything made that hath been made." It is further stated, on a line with the second verse of the Epistle, "In him was life"; and life is here brought into a relation with light — "and the life was the light of men" — which we shall learn to appreciate fully only after the discussion of a later topic (pp. 162 *seq.*). But even now we can very well understand the expression in so far as it affirms that the Word was also the medium of revelation. This thought is continued down to verse 14: "The light shineth in the darkness; and the darkness apprehended it not" 1 5. The Baptist as a mere witness is distinguished from the true light 1 6-8. "*The* true light, which lighteth every man, was coming into the world. He was in the world, and the world was made through him, and the world knew him not. He came unto his own, and his own received him not" 1 9-11. It is here affirmed that corresponding to the universal relation which the Logos has to the world as its creator, he is also universally the mediator of revelation. But he can particularly claim the Jewish people as "his own" on the ground of his special revelation to them through the Old Testament prophets; as by the acceptance of the revelation which he personally brings, men become truly the children of God 1 12.

In all this there are substantially but three assertions which are not included in Jesus' self-witness, nor expressed with reference to the Son of God. The first: oneness of nature with God, is, as we have seen, the particular point of S. John's belief which prompted the invention of such a designation as the Word. The second and third: participation in the creation, and mediation in the revelation of truth, were on the other hand not improbably suggested by the name Word itself. We shall see in another place, where we discuss in detail the relation of the Prologue to the first chapter of Genesis (pp. 113 *seq.*), how near lay the suggestion of attributing to the personal Word of God the act of creation. In the idea of Son there was already included the special fitness to interpret the Father's nature and will, and this was a pre-eminent factor of Jesus' claim; but it is not unlikely that this very name which S. John chose to designate the Son of God as pre-incarnate first brought to expression in his own mind the idea that he was in old time also the medium of revelation; — that he in fact was the Word which came to the prophets.

The Word which was in the beginning with God, and participated in God's work of creation and revelation, is brought into relation with the historical Christ in the simple affirmation, " *The Word became flesh* " 1 14. With this however we pass from the subject of this section to the Logos as manifested in the world; — a theme which we shall have to postpone to page 118 *seq.*

III

THE KOSMOS LYING IN DARKNESS

THE WORLD AS THE SPHERE OF HUMAN LIFE

S. JOHN conceives very vividly the contrast between the divine nature and the created world. As God is light, and in the light; so is the world characterised by darkness. But this contrast, strongly as it is marked, has no point of contact with philosophic dualism; for "darkness" is an ethical conception, and the world which S. John has in mind is not the material universe as such, but the sphere of human existence The slight interest which S. John shows in the material aspects of the world proves how utterly alien to his thought are the cosmological speculations which have been attributed to him as the motive of his so-called doctrine of the Logos. He needed no intermediary to bridge the gulf between the invisible God and the sensible world; for this was not the contrast which occupied his mind. Even human nature itself as it is physically constituted is not evil; and therefore the Logos, who is God and not a being of intermediate grade, can become flesh. God through the Logos created the world, and there is not anything which is excepted from this relationship of creature to Creator. There is therefore no radical opposition between the world as such and God; and even the

[margin: S. John's Slight Interest in the Material Aspects of the World]

world of human existence which has fallen into rebellion against him is the object of his love and saving effort. The world is not the sphere in which God ordinarily dwells; but it is a sphere into which he can come, and in which he may even dwell (tabernacle) for a time 1 9 10 14. There is nothing to suggest that S. John departed in any respect from the common Biblical view of the world. There is very little in his writings which bears upon this question, because it simply was not a subject of interest to him.

There is another contrast in which the world is involved, and that too is the familiar Old Testament contrast of heaven and earth. These two spheres are contrasted not only in character, but in space, as "above" and "below" 8 23, in harmony with the constant representation of the Old Testament; — "heaven above and the earth beneath" Deut. 5 8. The lower world he also calls "this world" (ὁ κόσμος οὗτος) 8 23 in contrast to the higher, or heavenly world; though the name world itself usually suffices to denote the sphere of human existence in distinction from heaven in which God is 16 28 17 11 13. S. John is consistent and thorough with his representation of above and below; it is doubtless more than a figure of speech. The Spirit 1 32, the angels 1 51 and the Son of man 3 13 31 6 33 38 41 *seq.* 50 *seq.* 58 62 are represented as descending (καταβαίνειν, ἄνωθεν ἔρχεσθαι) from heaven, and their return is an ascent (ἀναβαίνειν). Heaven is not only separated in space from the earth, but is itself conceived in truly Jewish fashion in terms of space. In the Father's house are "many mansions" in which Jesus on his return thither will pre-

Sidenote: Heaven and Earth

pare a place for his disciples 14 ²; and this probably indicates the Biblical conception of heaven as a place characterised by many grades. About the constitution of heaven S. John does not however speculate any more than he does about the constitution of the earth: the religious interest is everything to him, and heaven and earth are only the sphere in which the drama of salvation is enacted.

The contrast between God and the world, between darkness and light, just because it is an ethical contrast, is one of prime importance to S. John, and affects the whole scheme of his representation. Both heaven and earth are represented in Gen. 1 ₁ as equally the creation of God; and S. John doubtless comprises them both in the third verse of the Prologue: "All things were made through him; and without him was not anything made which was made." He does not however so much think of them as constituting one universe, but rather as exhibiting the moral contrast which has come about within God's creation; and he thinks of the world as an object requiring salvation out of the evil and darkness into which it has fallen. Darkness, as an ethical condition, could not have been the original and necessary character of the world: it came about as an historical development, and (as we shall see on page 108 *seq.*) in no other way than that which is represented in the Book of Genesis, namely, through sin. But, however it came about, darkness is the character of the world as Jesus finds it. It is into a realm of spiritual darkness and death that he comes bringing light and life. This world, which as we have seen is simply the

The Material Chaos and the Ethical Darkness

totality of human nature, or the sphere of human life, S. John conceives, after the analogy of the chaos which preceded the material creation, as the object of God's saving work, the matter of a veritable new creation. Here too it is the same divine Word which effects the re-creation; the first boon which he brings is light (a spiritual light, "the light of men" 1 4); and this conditions all spiritual life.

THE DARKNESS

Important as this antithesis between God and the world certainly was in the development of S. John's thought, and absolutely as he expresses the fact that when Christ came as a light into the world he found it simply darkness, we cannot allow the absoluteness of this antithesis to determine in detail his conception of the state of mankind before the Incarnation. For in the first place, although "the darkness apprehended not the light" 1 5, "and his own received him not" 1 11; there were nevertheless those who did receive him 1 12, and before they became his they belonged to the Father 17 6. There were in fact already at his coming two classes of men: those who hate the light because they do evil, and those who come to the light because they do the truth 3 20 21. And Jesus' work consists in part in this, that he separates out of the darkness those who by God's choice and their own disposition are inclined to the light (see pp. 133 *seq.*). In the second place, S. John recognises in the Jewish Scriptures a revelation from God, and in the Jewish nation a peculiar relation to God and knowledge of Him.

[margin: The Revelation of the Old Covenant]

We have already interpreted the ninth verse of the Prologue to mean that the Logos is the medium of God's universal revelation of Himself to men, and that he was that even before his coming into the world. But at any rate to his chosen people God did give special revelations of his character and of his purpose, and the value of such revelation is shown pre-eminently in the fact that Christ himself is the subject of Old Testament prophecy. "Isaiah saw his glory, and he spake of him" 12 ^{41}; Moses wrote of him 5 ^{47} cf. 1 ^{45}, and also the prophets. The divine mission of John the Baptist 1 ^{6} is specially emphasised in the Fourth Gospel; though not the light 1 ^{8}, he nevertheless even as a witness to the true light was himself "the lamp which burneth and shineth" 5 ^{35}. S. John's interpretation of Caiaphas' counsel 11 ^{51} *seq.* shows very strikingly his conception of prophecy as the official distinction of the Jewish nation even in the moment when they were consummating the disruption of the covenant relation.

The Scriptures of the Old Testament possess a value as a revelation of truth quite apart from the fact that they contain the word of God spoken to the prophets: the various sacred writings are conceived of as a unit, as "the Scripture" (a term which is used to denote the Old Testament as a whole 7 ^{38}, and its individual utterances 19 ^{37}), and this Scripture "cannot be broken" 10 ^{35}. S. John is not one whit behind any other Apostle in his estimate of the worth and trustworthiness of the Scriptures, both in respect to the facts which they narrate, and to the revelation which they contain respecting God and Christ. His references to the Old Testament are hardly less numerous than those of S. Matthew, and he surpasses all other Evangelists in the emphasis which he lays upon the fulfilment of prophecy in Christ. The Scriptures as a whole testify of Christ 5 39, and this witness is found not only in passages which are expressly prophetic, but in the Psalms 19 24 28 37, and even in the Law 19 36 3 14. It is this prophetic character of the Scripture which had the predominant interest for S. John. So complete was the Scriptural prophecy of Jesus, that had the disciples really known the Scripture, they would have known what must happen to him 20 9. So too it was of course the prophetic character of Scripture which gave it its abiding worth for the Church. The word Law, on the other hand, is used to describe the Scriptures in respect to their significance for the Jewish nation. Christ in addressing the Jews speaks of "your Law" 8 17 10 35, and of " Moses' Law" 7 23, whereas in his use of the word Scripture there is no such expression of personal detachment. This, however, is not to be taken as a proof that Jesus repudiated the obligation of the Law for himself and for his disciples; for when he says, "Which of you convicteth me of sin?" 8 46 he must be understood as challenging comparison between his conduct and the Law; and even in the alleged cases of Sabbath-breaking he justifies his action by a right interpretation of the Law 7 22. Neither is it to be supposed that S. John, distinguishing sharply between the two principal divisions of the Scripture, the Law and the Prophets, honors the one and rejects the other; for in Philip's call to Nathanael 1 45 the two are most intimately combined; —"of whom Moses in the Law, and the Prophets did write." S. John did not even, like S. Paul, think of the Law as the fundamental contrast to the Gospel. The contrast expressed in 1 17 is Pauline only in form: "For the Law was given by Moses; grace and truth came by Jesus Christ." Here the Law is supposed to be a thing good in itself, or the peculiar excellence of the gift of Christ would not be made to appear by the comparison. The point of the comparison is suggested by the preceding verse, "Of his fulness we have all received, and grace for grace." It is as the inexhaustible gift of God that the Gospel is contrasted with the Law, which, whatever its excellence, came not in the guise of a gift, but of a requisition. It is true that the term Law did not express to the Christian, as it did to the Jew, the predominant note of religion: and this usage which we note in S. John is precisely that which was natural in the age in which he wrote;—when the Jews clung to the Old Testament as Law, while the Church valued it as Scripture. Nor is there reason to think it unnatural in the mouth of Christ, since the constant trend of his teaching was away from the legalising spirit which dominated Judaism.

It seems natural to suppose that the Jews, to whom God had from time to time made revelations of Himself, to whom His Prophets even then came, and who had in the Scriptures a veritable witness to Him, must be accounted to have some knowledge of God before Christ came to them; and in fact Christ does allow that they have such knowledge, at least, in contrast with the Samaritans 4 22. It seems therefore hard to account for the absoluteness of S. John's judgment of the world as dark-

The Jews in the Fourth Gospel

ness at the appearing of Christ. We cannot dismiss this as an exaggeration of his antithetical mode of thought; nor can we suppose that such knowledge as the Jews had was simply outshone by the brightness of the coming light, or overlooked in the thought of the universality of surrounding darkness; for the Gospel does not represent the Jews as merely included in the darkness, but as the very representatives of it.

The rôle which is accorded the Jewish opponents of Jesus, is in fact one of the most prominent peculiarities of the Fourth Gospel, and constitutes a problem which is justly accounted of great importance. From beginning to end of the Gospel, S. John's representation moves on the lines of this opposition between Christ and the Jews 1 17, 20 19 and 7 & 8; and it requires but a glance to see that in it is summed up that opposition of the world to Christ which makes his very being in the world a conflict with the world 16 33. This conflict with the Jews conditions so thoroughly S. John's whole representation, that it has been singled out as the special aim of the Fourth Gospel. This however it cannot be, in view of S. John's express declaration in 20 31 (see page 25 *seq.*). On the other hand it is not sufficiently explained by a reference to the author's literary peculiarity, his preference for antithetical expression; nor does the Jewish unbelief serve merely as the dark background which throws into stronger relief the picture of Jesus' divine glory. Either case would presume a certain indifference on the part of the author to the fate of the Jewish nation. The problem strictly is this: What significance are we to attach to the Evangelist's employment of the

Jews as the representatives of the unbelieving world? If the problem is rightly expressed in this form, it shows how insufficient is the apparently near-lying answer, that it was *as a matter of fact* Jewish unbelief with which Jesus had to contend. For the peculiarity of S. John's representation is not that it was with the Jews Jesus had to deal, but that it was the Jewish people as such which opposed itself to Jesus' revelation, and brought to manifestation the alienation of the world from God and the hate of the darkness for the light. That is plainly enough expressed in the general name *the Jews* under which S. John as a rule represents the antagonists of Jesus; — without marking their individuality more particularly. This use of the national name to denote indiscriminately the various opponents of Jesus, is in contrast with the Synoptic account; and it is doubtless referable in part to the fact that S. John was addressing readers to whom the distinction between the Jewish religious parties was no longer familiar. But it cannot be taken to indicate that the author himself was unfamiliar with the precise conditions within the Jewish nation in the time of Christ. For hand in hand with this summary treatment of the Jews as the opponents of Jesus, there runs through the whole Gospel a representation of the individual elements with which he had to deal. S. John distinguishes in a very characteristic way between the rulers and the people, 7 $_{25}$ *seq.* 48 *seq.* 18 $_{35}$, between Jews, Galileans and Pereans, between the easily moved multitude which the feasts brought together in Jerusalem, and the proper inhabitants of Jerusalem 7 $_{20\ 25}$. No Evangelist is better informed than he about the recognition which Jesus received from all classes of the nation, from the lowest to the highest; and about the applause which he received when for the moment he seemed to realise the Messianic expectation 11 48 12 19. He makes it plain, too, that it was not so much the masses of the people that opposed him; as the rulers, the official representatives of the nation 7 48 49. Of this ruling class he mentions, now the Pharisees, now the high-priests, and again both together, as the recognised heads of the nation, and as coming together in Sanhedrim to pronounce an official judgment. This very specification, however, serves to render more definite the fact that in picturing the opposition of the Jews S. John is following a tendency which is calculated to represent the apostasy of the nation.

If we must acknowledge such a tendency, there are but two possible explanations of its motive: in the manner in which the Evangelist speaks of the Jews, he manifests the most uncompromising anti-judaism; or he betrays, by the very interest which he bestows upon this trait of his composition, his personal interest in the Jewish nation and in its fate.

In spite of the fact that the anti-judaism of the Fourth Gospel has been so loudly contended for, and has so seriously prejudiced the question of its authorship, there is in fact no expression in the Gospel of ill-will against the Jews;—nothing even which could match the "woes" recorded by the Synoptists. It cannot be claimed that there is in S. John's account any exaggeration of the hostility which Jesus actually encountered from the Jews. We learn also from the Synoptists that the Jews were less ready to believe than the Galileans, who were not so directly under the influence of the scribes and priests who gave the dominant tone to Judaism; and the Jewish opposition comes in for more extended notice in the Fourth Gospel, because the author has chosen to dwell particularly upon the episodes of Jesus' ministry in Judea. On the contrary there is frequent reference to belief among the Jews, extending even to the highest circles 12 42. The resurrection of Lazarus leads "many Jews" to faith in Jesus, 11 45, and to a definite separation from his opponents 12 11. Even the covert faith of Nicodemus and of Joseph of Arimathæa comes finally to public expression 3 2 19 38 39. And S. John recognises that it is primarily in "this fold" that Jesus finds his sheep 10 16.

If the hypothesis of anti-judaism proves itself insufficient to account for the whole problem we are considering, the other alternative must receive its due recognition. There is no lack of positive support for the view that the Evangelist regards with personal interest, even with intimate sympathy, the fate which overtook the Jewish nation in consequence of its attitude towards Jesus. (I follow here very closely, as I have followed more freely throughout this paragraph, the exposition of Franke: "Das alte Testament bei Johannes," page 17 *seq.*). Even in the earliest expression which denotes the rôle accorded to the Jews in the Fourth Gospel 1 11, the Evangelist speaks of the rejection of the Logos by "his own" (οἱ ἴδιοι) as of a fact of tragic significance. And the retrospect of 12 37 *seq.* shows that he stood before the unbelief of the nation as before a problem which was only then solved for him when he found the doom of the covenant people predicted in the words of the

Prophet. Even then, however, he looks back to the fact that faith was actually present, though not decided enough to endure the separation from the Synagogue. As moreover in another passage it is rejection from the Synagogue which deters from a free confession of Jesus 9 $_{22}$, or results from it 9 $_{34}$ *seq.*; so in the prophetic word which is quoted in 16 $_2$ one detects plainly enough what was the trial which the Evangelist found hardest of all the hardship which the following of Jesus brought with it 12 $_{25}$ 15 $_{18}$ 16 $_{33}$ 17 $_{14}$ I. 3 $_{13}$; — namely, the breach with the Synagogue, which was therefore most surely the home of his religious life. Then however he as well as S. Paul was a Hebrew of the Hebrews Phil. 3 $_5$ II. Cor. 11 $_{22}$, and in the one case no more than in the other can we speak of anti-judaism. The same fact which appeared to S. Paul the great mystery of the economy of grace, Rom. 11 $_{25}$, is also for S. John the highest problem of the history of salvation: the fact that a congregation of believers out of all the world, without reference to race, enjoys salvation in Christ, while the covenant people remains shut out from it. He however, looking back from a more advanced development of history, sees the fact more clearly than S. Paul, and speaks not merely of a partial and temporary rejection of Israel, but undertakes to show how, in the place of the ἴδιοι, the Old Testament people of God's possession, in whose midst Jesus appeared, I $_{11}$, another congregation of ἴδιοι had been constituted 13 $_1$; and, on the ground of a common faith, not of a common lineage, had become God's children, I $_{12}$ *seq.*

We see, therefore, that S. John's treatment of the

Jews as the representatives of the darkness of the world does not imply any prejudice against their original covenant relation to God, nor against their actual reception of revelation in time gone by, and present possession of it in the Scripture. Christ affirms that "salvation is of the Jews," 4 22; he asserts that if they were truly Abraham's children, they would do the works of Abraham 8 39; that if they had believed Moses, they would have believed him 5 46; and that the very Scriptures upon which they rely, bear testimony to him 5 39. The Jews therefore are characterised as darkness, not because no light has shone upon them, but because the light has not penetrated them. Light and darkness are ideas which lie strictly in the moral and not in the intellectual plane. The light does not illuminate mechanically from the outside, it demands rather a willing acceptance into the heart. The darkness therefore which rejected the light of the Logos remained none the less darkness because he had shone upon it. It was of the Jews of his own time that Jesus affirmed, "Ye have neither heard his voice at any time, nor seen his face" 5 37; — specifying the two forms in which God's revelation came in old time: by vision and by voice. But not only does no new revelation come to them; they do not even understand the Scriptures which they have inherited and which they study 5 39 40, and hence they do not receive the witness which the Father bears to the Son 5 37, because God's word finds no abiding-place in them 5 38. As they are unable to perceive God's witness, so they do not understand Christ's speech, because they cannot hear his word 8 43.

Since it is in the rejection of Jesus that the darkness of the world comes to pre-eminent expression, we realise that for S. John, unbelief is the superlative of sin. The Jews are regarded as the representatives of the evil power of the darkness in its struggle against the light, not because they were peculiarly distinguished for sensual sins and overt transgressions of God's Law, but because they refused to receive the light. Christ's coming into the world is itself a judgment, and the decision which men make for or against him, lays bare the inmost disposition of the heart;— "and this is the judgment, that light is come into the world, and men loved darkness rather than light; for their works were evil" 3 19. Unbelief is not a category which includes all sins; but it is the test which cuts deepest, and which most conclusively manifests the bent of the heart. The rejection of the light is not only significant in itself as a moral preference for darkness; but it further argues an evil life in the man who shuns the light 3 20 21. So predominant is this idea of sin that Jesus says, "If I had not come and spoken unto them, they had not had sin: but now they have no excuse for their sin. He that hateth me hateth my Father also. If I had not done the works which none other did, they had not had sin: but now they have both seen and hated both me and my Father" 15 22-24. And when at the last he promises that "the Paraclete will convict the world in respect of sin," he defines the sin of the world in the clause, "of sin, because they believe not in me" 16 8 9 The sin of the antichrist is variously stated as the denial "that Jesus Christ is come in the flesh" I. 4 2

Sin

II. 7, " that Jesus is the Christ " I. 2 22, or as the denial " of the Father and the Son ; " in any case it concerns this crucial attitude of unbelief, which is the sin *par excellence* for S. John. In the same way, in accordance with this characteristic of S. John, we must understand the " sin unto death " I. 5 16 17. We cannot understand it as anything other than a deliberate apostasy from Christ which involves a definitive crisis of the soul. It is the sin not of the outsider, but of the " brother " who has seen Christ and hated him.

S. John does not however confine himself to the consideration of the sin of unbelief; In the last passage which we quoted he contrasts sin unto death with sin in general: " All unrighteousness is sin ; and there is a sin not unto death " I. 5 17. The expression, " sin is lawlessness," which we find in the Epistle 3 4, shows his fundamental adherence to the Old Testament conception of sin. Sin is therefore not limited to those who are guilty of the overt act of denial of Christ 15 22; even those to whom the manifestation of Christ's light has not come are in a state of sin ; for it is into a world already sinful that Christ comes, " to take away the sin of the world " 1 29 I. 3 5. It is a world completely sinful; for sin is co-extensive with the darkness, and it is expressly stated of the world, after the Christian community has been separated from it, that it " lieth all of it in the Evil One " I. 5 19. The condition of sin is compared to bondage 8 34. Sin is in a negative sense death (the absence of life), and it is only by faith that we pass out " of death into life " 5 24 I. 3 14. It is out of a perishing condition Christ saves us 3 16. In a certain sense it is natural for men to sin; for, in a way quite familiar to the Old Testament, the pleasures of the world are regarded as enticements away from God. "For all that is in the world, the lust of the flesh, and the lust of the eyes, and the vainglory of life, is not of the Father, but of the world" I. 2 16. Flesh however is not thought of as an evil principle, any more than is the eye; nor can we take Christ's sentence in 3 6, "That which is born of the flesh is flesh," as an expression of the necessary sinfulness of humanity, for it means only that the earth-born is unable to transcend the earthly sphere without a begetting from above. Neither is the world itself to be considered evil by virtue of its physical constitution; for it is the creation of the Logos. S. John does nevertheless trace back all particular acts of sin to a single principle of sinfulness, and finally to the Devil himself, who rules in the world 14 30, and whom Christ comes to cast out 12 31.

S. John uses both the noun *sin* (ἁμαρτία) and the verb *to sin* (ἁμαρτάνειν) in two senses: to denote the power or principle of sin, or to denote concrete acts of sin. The latter sense he generally expresses by the plural, sins; but it is not always possible to distinguish which idea is uppermost in his thought. This distinction helps in part to explain how in the Epistle he can denounce the claim of sinlessness 1 8, and yet assert that "he that sinneth hath not seen him, hath not known him" 3 6. The Christian even is often guilty of particular acts of sin for which confession and forgiveness is required; but as he has been freed from the bondage of sin 8 36, and is no longer under its slavish control, he cannot habitually practise it, nor abide in it, still less can he be guilty of sin in its superlative form, by denial of Christ. We have seen also that sin is lawlessness I. 3 4, and in that expression there lies a conception more peculiar to S. John than at first appears; for law is no longer presented in the form of many precepts, but summed up in Christ's example of love. As sin against God is thought of chiefly as rejection of his light, so all sin against man is included in the idea of hate, the transgression of the law of love. This sin is traced back to Cain " who was of the Evil One, and slew his brother" I. 3 12. It is likely that S. John did not think so much of the unity of the sinful race as derived from Adam, as of the moral contrast within the race, between the children of God and the children of the Devil; of this contrast Cain was the representative, and his sin was for S. John the antitypal sin.

But even Cain's sin is traced to the fact that he was of the Evil One, who himself " was a murderer from the beginning," 8 44. " He that doeth sin is from the Devil, for the Devil sinneth from the beginning" I. 3 8. Christ says to the Jews: " Ye are of your father the Devil, and the lusts of your father it is your will to do" 8 44. As to the origin of the Devil himself, we can simply say that S. John shows no sign that he speculated at all about it. And if he did not speculate about it, it is difficult to believe that he departed so far from the common doctrine of the Church as to represent the Devil as in any sense coordinate with God, as the eternal principle of evil. Notwithstanding an expression like that we have just quoted, which seems to represent a derivation of nature from him, he is simply the tempter, as we see in the case of Judas 13 2. And although S. John does thus dwell upon the contrast within the human race between the children of God and the children of the Devil, although he often represents the difference between them as something which antedated their conscious choice of Jesus 10 3 5 16; we cannot find here a metaphysical distinction between the two classes, which necessitates their relation to Christ. For, in thorough keeping with the Old Testament, this difference is traced to God's choice, they were his before they were Christ's 17 6; and yet their own choice remains one of perfect freedom, expressing the character of their will. It is because men love darkness rather than light, that they reject Christ and are therefore justly judged 3 19. In 9 41 the maxim is expressed, that physically necessitated action, even if it amounted to the rejection of Jesus, cannot be accounted sin: "If ye were blind, ye would have no sin: but now ye say, We see: your sin remaineth."

IV

THE LIFE MANIFESTED

PARALLEL WITH THE FIRST CHAPTERS OF GENESIS

WE have now before us the two great generic ideas of Darkness and Light, which represent the contrast between the human and the divine, between God and the world. We have been able with reasonable certitude to deduce even from S. John's indirect utterances, his view of the nature and disposition of God, and of the condition of the world. But fundamental as these topics are, they are only the introduction to the themes with which S. John most expressly and predominantly deals. Light and Darkness, as we have come to understand them, are in a sense the postulates of S. John's theology: they are the colours with which his picture is painted. The contrast involved in these two facts represents also the problem which S. John's doctrine solves. But the all-absorbing fact to S. John is not that the world lieth in darkness, nor even that God is light; but that the divine light has actually come into the darkness. He sees the world perishing in darkness and death; he sees God as one who is light and in whom is no darkness at all: but he does not speculate upon these two facts, he does not even strive to delineate them, he is content to *name* them in two words.

What he does describe minutely, what he dwells upon almost exclusively, is the process by which the light, entering into the darkness, overcomes it and saves the world. The proposition that "God is light" does not merely express the immanent nature of God; but also the fact that, as it is the very nature of light to shine, so it is God's nature to manifest himself. The "heavenly things" which Jesus reveals — in contrast to the "earthly things" which the teacher of Israel might be supposed to know — are summed up in this: "*God so loved the world, that he gave his only begotten Son, that whosoever believeth on him should not perish, but have eternal life*" 3 16. It is the Logos become flesh, the life and the light manifested in the world, the Messiah come to save the world, eternal life, the new birth, the conditions and fruits of divine sonship; — it is with these themes that S. John is constantly occupied; and upon them the great majority of his utterances in both Epistle and Gospel directly bear. This is the region of Johannine doctrine with which we have yet to deal; and here it is we find the most obvious as well as the most interesting of the Johannine peculiarities.

Before we proceed more closely to the study of this section, we must examine the highly interesting parallel which exists between the Prologue of the Gospel and the first Chapters of the Book of Genesis. Some features of this parallel we have already had occasion to note; some of them are suggested at the very first glance; but the parallel extends much further and more into detail than is commonly supposed. Its importance at this point is that it helps us to realise S. John's thoroughly objective, one might almost say pictorial, conception of the sphere and operation of redemption; and that it furnishes luminous points of suggestion for the construction of this chapter of Johannine thought.

The first hint of this relation of thought is the very first phrase of the Gospel, "In the beginning." This could scarcely have been written without a reminiscence of the first words of the Old Testament Scripture; and it obviously suggests that the author is about to write a second Book of Genesis, an account of a new creation. If we have in the Prologue a *parallel* with Genesis, the phrase, "in the beginning," must in the two instances denote not the same, but a different *time;* it is therefore worth while observing that the word "beginning" in S. John's use commonly refers to the commencement of the Gospel dispensation, to the time of the appearance of Christ 16 4 I. 2 7 24 II. 56. The several ideas which are common to the first chapters of Genesis and to the Prologue are: the creative Voice — the Word; the light and the darkness; and the various manifestations of life. It is a question rather curious than grave, whether "the Spirit of God" in Gen. 1 5 is not another point of contact with the Gospel re-creation; but it is at least not at all improbable that Christ's act of breathing out the Holy Spirit upon his disciples 20 22 was associated in S. John's mind with God's breathing into man the breath of life as recounted in Gen. 2 7. We may account it likely that S. John's idea of eternal life was associated with "the Tree of Life;" and it is possible that his close association of knowledge and life has some connection with the two trees of the Garden (see the Apocalypse for this and other analogies with the terrestrial Paradise). With these common ideas as the subject-matter, the parallel is worked out as follows. In Genesis we are directed to God as the Creator of the heavens and the earth. Before us lies a material chaos enveloped in darkness; into which presently at the utterance of the creative word shines the light;—which appears later in concrete manifestation as "lights." The creation proceeds by the instrumentality of the Word to effect a still further division, of the waters from the waters, and of the waters from the land. The first part of creation is thus effected by means of simple mechanical separation; further development is wrought by the introduction of the various stages of life;—from the green herb to the beast wherein is a living soul. Man is not only the climax of this order of living souls; but he is constituted a different kind by the breath of God. This supreme and unique product of creation proceeds, according to the divine command, to multiply and fill the earth.

The world for S. John is, as we have repeatedly remarked, simply the dwelling-place of mankind, the sphere of human souls. This psychical sphere has been thrown by sin into a state of spiritual chaos; it is under the power of darkness and of the Evil One; and hence it is the object of salvation, which S. John thinks of as a new creation. Accordingly, quite parallel with Genesis, his description takes for its "beginning" the commencement of the re-creation. "*In* the beginning," in timeless duration extending back from this point, we are pointed to the Word, who was with God, who was God. He is disclosed as the original Creator of all things. As in Genesis "the earth was without form and void, and darkness was upon the face of the deep;" so here there lies before us a spiritual chaos which is enveloped in spiritual darkness. As in Genesis the first moment of creation is the creative word, "Let there be light," so here the Word is the personal Creator, and he also was light; — a spiritual light, the light of men. By him a separation is effected between the different elements of the world, and order is brought out of chaos. We shall see subsequently (pp. 130 *seq.*) how thoroughly regulative of his thought, and even of the order of his narrative, is this idea of the division which the very appearance of Christ as the light brings about among men. But not only was he light; "in him was life." He brings eternal life to men, and this as we shall see is thought of, not as a mere prolongation of physical existence which would else be broken off by death, but as an entirely new and superadded gift, which has its beginning in the new birth. This new birth ("not of bloods, nor of the will of the flesh, nor of the will of man, but of God") is parallel to the first divine gift of psychical life in Gen. 2 7. This life consists in the felicity of knowledge of and fellowship with God: it is truly possessed from the moment of the new birth, but there is a development of it corresponding to the development in knowledge. The detailed process of the production of physical life in Genesis, has its counterpart in the development of this one life; just as the separate moments of creation are here blended in the continuous operation of the personal Word. A glance at the table of contents (pages vi and vii) will show how these guiding principles of thought are wrought out in S. John's doctrine;—for it is not only the Prologue, but the whole Gospel, which S. John, in the terms of this introduction, would set forth as a second Book of Genesis.

THE WORD BECOME FLESH

Before we study the effects produced in the world by the coming of the Word, we must consider what was involved in the very fact of this "*coming*" out of the heavenly into the earthly sphere. In 1 14 we have the summary expression, "the Word became flesh." This is not meant as a complete and formal definition of the act whereby the Logos came into relation with humanity; for this has actually been the theme of the preceding verses, and is expressed generally in the simple word "came." But by this phrase is expressed the fact that in coming amongst men, he became what all men are: namely, flesh. The image of the following phrase, "tabernacled among us," might suggest that the Logos merely dwelt in a human body, as a form of manifestation. But to become flesh means something more than to assume a body: Flesh is human nature, it is always animated flesh, the seat of the human soul; and to *become* means actually to be something one was not before. S. John, however, presents us with no theory; he has merely *data* to set before us. What could be more thoroughly a *datum* of his experience than the fact that Jesus was man; whatever theorising he did on this subject, was not to represent how the Logos became man, but how the man Jesus was God.

<small>The Nature of the Incarnation</small>

In spite of the fact that S. John in the very Prologue lets us into the secret of Jesus' divine nature, and that he composes his Gospel with the distinct purpose of establishing belief in him as the Son of God; he nevertheless dramatises him before us as man. As a man he appears in the familiar relations of family life: with his mother and his brethren he attends a wedding, evidently within the circle of his friends or relatives 2 12; he abides for a time in the family circle at Capernaum 2 12; his brethren even undertake to lecture him about his conduct 7 3-8; and from the cross he displays his care for his mother 19 25 26. As a man Jesus wept at the grave of Lazarus, 11 35; he was troubled in soul at the thought of death 12 27; and shows even a momentary hesitation whether he shall not pray to be delivered from this hour. In 8 40 he actually calls himself a man. But his truly human consciousness is expressed nowhere so clearly as in his relation to God. Notwithstanding the exalted character of his self-witness, in his human existence he bears even to the Father the relation of a man to God 20 17; he prays to his Father 12 27 and chapter 17; he thanks him for his gifts 6 11, and also for hearing his petitions 11 41. Though S. John thinks of the Logos as the Creator of all things, he represents the miracles of Jesus, not as proceeding from his own inherent power, but as given him by the Father, in answer to his prayer, and for a special occasion 11 22 41 5 36 14 10. When Jesus says that he seeks not his own will, but the will of him that sent him 5 30 6 37, he postulates the double possibility of following his own human will, or the will of God. When he says

The Son of Man

that he seeks not his own honor, but that of his Father 8 49 50, he implies that the mastering of self-will and self-gratification was for him, as for other men, a moral task. The Father's will is expressed for him, as it is for other men, as an external will, as a "commandment," 12 49 50; and his life therefore like that of other men lies under the stress of obligation; — he includes himself with his disciples under the ethical *must*: "We must work the works of him that sent me," 9 4 R. V. This, however, is no irksome duty, for the fulfilment of his Father's will is his greatest joy 4 34.

To express the fact of Christ's truly human condition, S. John like the Synoptists uses Jesus' self-chosen name "the Son of man." And this name is peculiarly significant, for it expresses not only the fact that Christ was a man among men, but that his original condition was something quite different; for the name would have no force as applied to one who self-evidently and as a matter of course was man and nothing else. The passage (Dan. 7 13) which suggested Christ's use of this name, expressed also the thought that this Son of man was from heaven, and was to establish upon earth an everlasting kingdom. S. John shows at least that this reference was understood by the Jews, for they are offended at Jesus' allusion to the departure of the Son of man from the earth 12 34; — an idea apparently so contrary to the Scriptural prophecy. The name "Son of man" was capable however of representing something more than the common Messianic doctrine; and in two passages in particular its peculiar significance is very clearly marked. In 5 27 Jesus says that the

Father gave the Son authority to execute judgment, "because he is the Son of man." The judgment which is here spoken of consists in this, that some hear, while others do not hear Christ's word 5 $_{24\ 25}$. This implies that he is a son of man whose word can be heard and apprehended, and because he is this, because he comes into this real relation with men, God gives him authority of judgment — *cf.* 3 $_{19}$. In the discourse of the sixth chapter concerning the true bread of life which comes down from heaven, we see that it is as Son of man that Jesus gives this bread 6 $_{27}$. This meat from heaven can be brought only by the Son of man who himself also is from thence; and it can be imparted to men only by one who like him comes into relation with men. Moreover, as the highest revelation of God is given in Christ's loving sacrifice upon the cross, through which it becomes possible that men may eat his flesh and drink his blood 6 $_{53}$, it is clear that only as his is a true human life can it be relinquished in death; and on the other hand, that only as he is the highest revelation of God can his death impart life.

The word Messiah, like every other name which was employed to express the position of the Logos in his earthly manifestation, was used also to express his higher relationship. The Messianic idea (expressed not only under the title "the Christ," but also under other terms) is as common in the Fourth Gospel as in any other; and the Fourth Gospel more clearly than any other furnishes the clue to the process by which the popular Messianic doctrines, which at first disposed the people to welcome Jesus, turned them subsequently to enmity,

The Messiah

and finally brought about the national rejection of a Messiah who corresponded so poorly to their dogmatic preconceptions. It is charged however that S. John has suffered the idea of the Messiah, and its corollary the kingdom of God, to fall into the background; and has superseded it with the higher conceptions involved in the terms, Logos and Son. The importance, however, which the Messianic hope had for him is shown generally by the fact that Jesus' constant conflicts with the Jews revolved about this subject. And the fact that Jesus is therein represented as repudiating the Messianic notions of the Jews, cannot indicate on the part of the author either indifference or opposition to the Messianic idea itself; for we see also in the Synoptic Gospels that Jesus' whole ministry was occupied in raising to a higher plane the popular conceptions of the Messianic King and his kingdom. We cannot fail to note the zeal with which S. John throughout his whole Gospel pursues the proof of Jesus' Messianic character; from the witness of the Baptist, to the circumstances of his passion. It certainly appears as if the Messianic problem had a special interest for him just because it was a Jewish question and involved the fate of the Nation. We cannot help noticing a joyful note in the Evangelist's reminiscence of those first days which (as the unnamed disciple) he passed with Jesus I 40: and the key-note of those days was the glad assurance, "we have found the Messiah" I 42. Nor did this name, much as it must have gained in significance, become old and out of date; for he uses this title in the Epistle, and expresses the very aim of his Gospel in this, "that ye may believe that

Jesus is the Christ, the Son of God." We must perforce forbear to pursue in detail the Messianic question in the Fourth Gospel. The discussion, minute and prolonged as it would have to be, would not contribute to our general appreciation of the Johannine theology. Apart from the subtle suggestions of criticism, one would unhesitatingly form the opinion that S. John had the same interest in the Messianic character of Jesus as had the other Evangelists. The title, Christ, never became with him a mere personal name, an adjunct of the name Jesus; but always retains its original force. He speaks, it is true, of "Jesus Christ;" but always with the significance of Jesus the Messiah. Although it is true that the confession which in the Epistle is emphatically made the test of orthodoxy — "that Jesus Christ is come in the flesh" — is directed especially against the Gnostic denial that the heavenly *aeon* Christ was identical with the man Jesus; yet it at least includes the assertion of his real Messianic character. . Jesus does not expressly say to the world "I am the Christ;" but neither does he do so in the Synoptic accounts. When the Jews however asked him to tell them plainly, "if thou art the Christ," Jesus answered, "I told you, and ye believe not" 10 $_{24\ 25}$; — implying that this has been all along the substance of his claim. In the same manner he acknowledges Pilate's question, "Art thou a king then?" 18 $_{37}$. If S. John does not generally employ the Messianic title in connection with what is nevertheless fundamentally his Scriptural proof of Jesus' Messianic character, this may be very obviously explained by the fact that for his gentile readers the distinctly Messianic idea was of less interest than it was to the author himself, whereas the Scriptural legitimation in itself was still — as it has continued to be — of the liveliest interest. It remains to note the fact that Jesus' familiar word, "the kingdom of God," is recorded in only two passages of S. John's Gospel 3:3,5 18:36. This however only corresponds to the fact that this name did not remain in the Apostolic age a common designation of the Christian community. What may have been the causes which led to its disuse, we need not speculate; but there was at least one very obvious motive, namely, the fear of rousing the ready suspicion of the Roman Empire against the Church as a political faction (*cf.* 19:12). It is quite in accordance with the design of S. John's Gospel — which was an interpretation rather than a record — that he should omit even so striking a feature of Jesus' teaching; — or rather omit the *word*, in order that he might interpret the *thing* in terms familiar to his readers. On the other hand he uses the Messianic title of King more frequently and emphatically than any other evangelist. It is as "the King of Israel" that Nathanael hails him 1:49; as King that he makes his triumphal entrance into Jerusalem 12:13; and it is as King that he stands before the judgment-seat of Pilate, and as King is put to death.

We have seen that the Logos in his earthly manifestation condescended so to divest himself of his proper divine attribute of power, that even the signs which he performed were not manifestations of his creative omnipotence, but rather given him, or performed for him,

The Incarnation a Manifestation of the Glory of the Logos

by the Father. In coming into the world, he *descended* from heaven; and in a certain real sense was separated from God 3 16, and became subject like a creature to God's commandment, and to the ethical conditions of human life. The divine glory which he had with the Father before the creation of the world, and which was restored to him upon his ascension, he was deprived of in his earthly life 17 5. There was however no incompatibility in this contrast between the eternal glory and the earthly humility of the Logos; it was resolved very simply by the conception of the *mission* of the Son. This idea so common with S. John, "that the Father *sent* the Son," is used at once to express his subordination 7 18 *cf.* 3 16, and his exalted relation to the Father 8 16. The deprivation which he thereby suffered of the divine power and glory, was essential to the accomplishment of his mission as a man amongst men. But there were on the other hand certain possessions of his original state which he could not put away from him without defeating the very purpose of his mission. The Evangelist's comments upon Jesus' surprising knowledge of men, and of the events which were to complete his Messianic career 6 16 26 64 7 30 13 1 11 16 30 21 17, do not expressly ascribe to him divine omniscience, though they do declare that he was endowed with such insight as was requisite for his Messianic work. There was however one sort of knowledge which Jesus as the Revealer of God (in word as well as in work) must and did possess in no partial and creaturely way: that was *the knowledge of God*. His constant witness was to the effect that he possessed, as no other could possess, the perfect knowledge of God; and that this was derived, not from speculation, nor from prophetic inspiration, but from the reminiscence of that which he had *seen* in his intimate heavenly intercourse with the Father. Moreover, as the appreciation of his own nature was of essential importance to men, he must retain, and he did retain, a perfect self-consciousness of what he was and whence he came 8 14. Even this knowledge however he reveals to men only under the terms of his mission, as a commandment of his Father 12 49. As one who came also to impart life to men 10 10, he possessed life in an unique way; — "*in himself*" 5 26. This is associated with his possession of that perfect knowledge of God, which is a condition of eternal life; but he also claims the power "to take again," as he also of his own will "lay down," his human, physical life 10 18; — though this also he expresses as a "commandment received from my Father."

It is therefore not difficult to see why, in spite of facts which might justly be used to represent the earthly manifestation of the Son of God as a state of humiliation (as S. Paul thinks of it; — see especially Phil. 2 5-11), S. John does not think of it in this aspect. It is of the Word Incarnate, he says, "we beheld his glory, glory as of the only begotten from the Father" 1 14. And this, in connection with the expression "tabernacled," suggests the Shekinah, the glory with which God himself appeared among his people in the tent in the wilderness. It was in the man Jesus he had learned to know what God is, and his earthly manifestation he could not therefore regard as an obscuration of divinity, but as the only means whereby the divine character could be adequately manifested to men. The very fact that Jesus in his own person revealed God not so much in terms of might as of love, is proof that this is the most exalted attribute of God, his peculiar glory, and the very character of the light which is his nature I. 1 5. Because therefore the love of Christ was shown supremely in just those moments which from another point of view might be regarded as the very depths of his humiliation—his menial service 13 3-17, his betrayal, and his death—S. John regards them as the highest expression of his glorification among men;—which was at the same time a glorification of the Father 13 31. It is in short as the light of the world that Jesus appears in the world. And although S. John notices the obstacles of prejudice and misconception which hindered the Jews from believing upon him; he is nevertheless assured that even his earthly manifestation so clearly expressed his divinity, so clearly revealed him as light, that only those who were blinded by the darkness, or who wilfully turned away their eyes, could fail to see. To the proof of Jesus' divinity which the conscience ought to possess in the mere beholding of him, there is added Jesus' self-witness, the witness of the Baptist, and of the Scripture, and of the works which his Father gives him;—these also serve to glorify him, and to render it the more inexcusable that any should refuse to receive him for that which in his very nature he is, and which he manifests himself to be 12 40. It is the very clearness of the moral decision involved in the acknowledgment or the denial of Jesus which explains the position of the Son of man in the world at once as Saviour and as Judge.

A. SALVATION OUT OF THE WORLD

1. The Whole World as the Object of Salvation

One cannot fail to be struck with the universal reference which S. John's language attributes to Christ's saving work in the world. Not only is he in the world as Saviour; but he is sent as "the Saviour of the world" I. 4 14, and this sending is an expression of God's love for the world 3 16. The Baptist points to him as "the lamb of God, which taketh away the sin of the world" 1 29, and he himself testifies that he will give his flesh "for the life of the world" 6 51. This language is the more remarkable, because according to S. John's predominant use of this word in his Epistle, and Christ's uniform use of it in his last discourse with his disciples, it denotes, not the totality of human existence, but the evil remnant which is left after the Christian community has been gathered out. It is the evil world power, in contrast to the Church; it is not merely an unbelieving world, but a persecuting world 17 14 I. 3 13, which openly and violently displays its antagonism to Christ and to all who are his. S. John beholds the whole world lying in the Evil One I. 5 19. This indicates more than that subjection to darkness and sin which characterised the whole world at the coming of Christ: it has already seen and rejected Christ; it is therefore ripe for judgment 12 31, for the reproof of its sin of unbelief 16 8 9; and

Christ's attitude towards it is only that of conqueror 16 33; in that last hour he even forbears to pray for it 17 9, although he still looks forward to an ultimate turning of the world to belief through the ministry of his disciples 17 20, 21. It is of course not in this exclusive sense, denoting particularly the evil residue, that S. John uses the word when he speaks of the Logos coming into the world, and of Christ as the Saviour of the world: but it is in a sense which *includes* also this evil element; for it is the *whole world*. This universal reference is put beyond a doubt when he says, "*he is the propitiation for our sins; and not for ours only, but also for the whole world*" I. 2 2. It is not as though he were Saviour of both the good and the bad; for the whole world was in darkness and sin, and the discrimination of the two classes was subsequent to his manifestation, and a result of it, though not the purpose of it. Although Christ's manifestation in the world is actually a judgment, and although that which he actually accomplishes is in 9 39 represented as the purpose of his coming; there is really nothing in S. John's representation to contradict the solemn assertion: "*God sent not his Son into the world to condemn the world; but that the world should be saved through him*" 3 17 12 47. For Christ's judgment of the world consists simply in this, that God's loving gift of light to the world has as its inevitable consequence the revealing of the darkness, or rather, it presents the test which reveals the fundamental bent of every heart. "*And this is the judgment, that the light is come into the world, and men loved the darkness rather than the light*" 3 19. It is this figure of the light which again makes S. John's meaning clear and consistent. Jesus proclaims himself *the light of the world* 8 12 12 46, and in 9 5 he represents that being in the world, he must be its light. It is this perfectly objective mode of thought which explains S. John's meaning. Just as the light shines in the world, and shines none the less because the darkness apprehendeth it not; so, in the simplicity and directness of his thought, he beholds Jesus lying objectively before the world as the sacrifice and propitiation for its sin; and none the less *for* all — intended for all, available for all — that some do not accept the reconciliation which he offers. As the Baptist in early days pointed him to Jesus as " the lamb of God, which taketh away the sin of the world; " so finally he saw him hang upon the cross, " lifted up " before the eyes of the whole world, " as Moses lifted up the serpent in the wilderness," " that every one that believeth in him may have eternal life " 3 14 15.

2. THE DIVISION AMONGST MEN

The Fourth Gospel records no more striking saying of Jesus, considering the circumstances of its utterance, than that before Pilate and the rulers of the Jewish nation: " To this end have I been born, and to this end am I come into the world, that I should bear witness unto the truth. *Every one that is of the truth heareth my voice*" 18 37. At this word the apparent relationships in that hall of judgment are dissolved, inverted, and Jesus appears as Judge for the condemnation of his judge and of his accusers, who thereby proved that they were not of the truth, because they heard not his voice. It is characteristic of S. John that he represents the apostasy of the nation as culminating in the official act of its chiefs in delivering Jesus up to the Roman power. He does not record the extenuating words from the cross, "they know not what they do," Luke 23 34, nor in any wise admit that the rulers and people were acting in ignorance, Acts 3 17: it was the clear rejection, on the part of the nation and its rulers, of the Messianic King. It is rather Pilate whose conduct is pityingly extenuated on the ground that he exercises his power only subordinately 19 11, and under the dread of offending his master 19 12; whereas it is Jesus' own nation and the chief priests who delivered him unto him, who have the "greater sin," 18 35 19 11. This, as we have seen, is in accordance with S. John's constant representation, that the very manifestation of the truth (which is the light) is in itself the judgment of the world. In 8 43 Jesus says, "why do ye not understand my speech? *Even because ye cannot hear my word.*" This however is not a necessitated deafness, although it is traced back to the fact that the Devil is their father; for it is expressly said, "The lusts of your father it is your *will* to do" 8 44. Consistent with his claim that he is not in the world as Judge, though a judgment is accomplished by his presence, he says: "If any man hear my sayings, and keep them not, I judge him not; for I came not to judge the world, but to save the world. He that rejecteth me, and receiveth not my sayings, hath one that judgeth him: *the word that I spake, the same shall judge him in the last day*" 12 47 48. The judgment which is ascribed to Jesus' word, his truth, and his light, is in the above instances represented as a judgment of condemnation, for S. John uses the word almost always with this implication. In the third chapter, however, where he speaks of the judgment accomplished by the light, although the word is used simply in the sense of condemnation ("He that believeth is not judged: he that believeth not hath been judged already," 3 18 *cf.* 3 19,) he nevertheless notices the double effect of the light: upon them who *come* to it, as well as upon them who *hate* it 3 20 21. In another place he uses the word judgment itself in its original sense of mere discrimination; and denotes that the judgment which Christ is actually accomplishing in the world, is one which includes blessing as well as ban: "that they which see not may see; and that they which see may become blind" 9 39. This is parallel to the saying recorded by S. Luke: "not to give peace, but division" 12 51 *seq.* This reminds us that also according to the Synoptic account, Jesus' earthly manifestation in some sense forestalls the final judgment. But it is peculiarly characteristic of S. John, who thinks of the blessings of the Gospel (salvation and eternal life) as substantially present here and now, to think of the judgment also as virtually realised in the present. And this does not merely mean that the final judgment has only to pronounce upon the works already done on earth, Rev. 20 13; but the division itself, the segregation of the evil and the good, Mat. 25 32, is in some sort accomplished by Christ's manifestation upon earth. This idea of the division accomplished by Jesus amongst the men who heard his word, is one which to a very marked degree conditions the composition of the Fourth Gospel. Besides the passages upon which we have been commenting, there are no others so explicit of S. John's view; but we see that the whole Gospel is arranged with a view to demonstrate the diverse effects which the word of Jesus had upon his hearers, and to display the division which from the beginning of his ministry began to accomplish itself amongst men. It is hence expressly mentioned after many of his notable sayings or works, that "there arose a division among the multitudes concerning him" 7 43 9 16 10 19 *cf.* 7 12. This division proceeded even to a sifting of his own followers 6 66; Judas finally "went out" and left Jesus at last alone with his true friends 13 31. This sifting continued in the Apostolic Church; and the apostasy of its members was regarded as a sign that they had never really belonged to the community: "They went out from us, but they were not of us; for if they had been of us, they would have continued with us: but that they might be made manifest how that they all are not of us" I. 2 19.

The division which is thus accomplished in the world is not a mere incident of Christ's manifestation; it is, as regards the children of God, an essential step in the work of salvation. It has been already suggested that we may perhaps find here a parallel to the account of creation, according to which the mechanical division of the elements of the world preceded the production of life. At any rate it is a matter of real importance that the children of God should be separated from the evil elements of the world. It is especially in Jesus' final familiar discourse with his true friends, and in his prayer for them, that the contrast between the disciples and the world is expressed. Just as surely as they are "*in* the world" 13 1 17 11, just so surely are they "not *of* the world" 15 19. "They are not of the world even as I am not of the world" 17 16. And this is explained by the fact that he has chosen them (or that God has given them him 17 5) "*out* of the world" 15 19. At the end of his Epistle S. John expresses the vivid consciousness which the Christian community had of its separateness from the world: "We know that we are of God, and the whole world lieth in the Evil One" 5 19. There is more than a mere negative advantage in this separation of the children of God from the world; or rather this very act includes the formation of a Christian community, which can oppose itself as a unit to the world which itself is thought of as a unity represented in the person of the Prince of this world, and constitutes both a persecuting and a tempting power. The formation of a community out of the elements scattered abroad in the midst of the darkness of the world, is expressed in the saying, "that he might also gather together *into one* the children of God who are scattered abroad" 11 52. This is expressed also in the tenth chapter in Christ's parable of the shepherd. There too it is the *voice* of Christ which collects the flock, 10 5, and there are other sheep besides those of the Jewish fold which he must "*bring*" "and they shall become one flock, one shepherd" 10 16. This idea of unity is profoundly emphasised in Jesus' prayer, in which, looking into the future and beyond the circle of his present disciples, he entreats, "for them also who believe on me through their word; that they may all be one; as thou, Father, art in me, and I in thee, that they also may be in us: that the world may believe that thou didst send me" 17 $^{20, 21}$. We see from this quotation, and in general by a reference to the whole prayer, that this unity of the disciples is of the highest importance in manifold directions. In the first place, it is a positive good in itself, and the condition of fellowship with one another, and with God in Christ. It is further of importance, not only for protection against the world, and as a means of hostilely overcoming it; but as a means of gaining disciples out of the world, and even winning the world itself to faith. In this is seen the reason why, though Christ leaves the world, the disciples must remain in it; why they must be in it, though not of it; for Christ has sent them into the world, even as the Father sent him into the world 17 ^{18} *cf.* I. 4 ^{17}. We see therefore that this division which is brought about by the shining of the light of truth in the world, thereby gathering together into one the scattered children of God as against the collective might of darkness, is the first and fundamental effect of Christ's work of salvation, as regards both the individual and the community. Notwithstanding the mystical element of S. John's thought, and his vivid sense of personal union with Christ and God, salvation is not to be thought of apart from the community, which is the expression of separation out of the world and of adherence to Christ.

3. The Doom of the World

We have seen how slight a stress S. John lays upon the developments of the future; that he does not dwell upon the conceptions of *now* and *then*, but of here and there, above and below, heaven and earth. But nevertheless there lingers in his expression, "this world" (ὁ κόσμος οὗτος), the implication of another and a future world. He looks forward to Christ's *coming again* 14 ₃, which can only be understood, in the common New Testament sense, of the *Parousia*. And this coming is regarded not only with reference to his receiving of his own unto himself, but also as a judgment; for it requires a certain boldness and confidence to face him "at his coming" I. 2 ₂₈ — or as it is said in I. 4 ₁₇, "in the day of judgment" — which only they who abide in him, and are perfected in love, can possess. S. John's references to the "last day" and to "the day of judgment" are far too emphatic to allow us to suppose that they are merely occasional lapses into the language of the current representation which had however no place in the scheme of his own thought. The language which we considered under the last topic, concerning Christ's judgment as in a sense already accomplished, is very far from excluding — it rather presupposes — a future day of judgment. When Jesus asserts that he has come not to judge, but to save the world, he is expressly contradicting the Jewish expectation that the Messiah at his coming was to judge the world; in particular, to right the wrongs of his people, and execute vengeance upon their enemies. Jesus repudiates this interpretation of his mission, but he by no means denies the necessity of a definite judgment of mankind. The decisive sundering of the wicked from the righteous is essential to the idea of completed salvation; the Christian theology therefore retained the Jewish idea of the Messianic judgment, only it deferred it, as the developed situation demanded, to a second coming of the Messiah. When the Fourth Gospel represents that Christ by his very manifestation accomplishes a judgment which is not only a sentence upon, but in some measure a separation of, the faithful and the unbelieving; it cannot be supposed that a future act of judgment is thereby rendered superfluous; it is rather supposed by the whole character of this representation that Christ, who is not now here to perform judgment — although his very manifestation does in effect accomplish it — will perform it hereafter. For notwithstanding his denial that his present mission is one of judgment, Christ confirms the Jewish doctrine in so far as this, that judgment is a Messianic function. He claims that "the Father hath committed all judgment unto the Son" 5 22; and again, "he gave him authority to execute judgment, because he is the Son of man" 5 27. Even the special blessing which Christ imparts, the eternal life which S. John thinks of predominantly as a present possession, is not complete in itself, but requires still a special exercise of Christ's power in raising up the body at the last day 6 39-41 *cf.* 11 24 25. In 5 27-29 the judgment which is committed unto the Son of man, is expressly associated with the resurrection, "in which all that are in the tombs shall hear his voice, and shall come forth; they that have done good, unto the resurrection of life; and they that have done ill, unto the resurrection of judgment." Christ's word accomplishes a judgment upon earth; it is his word also which shall judge a man at the last day 12 48.

There is nothing to suggest that S. John's idea of the last day is in any way different from the conception which was common to Jewish and Christian theology. According to the Jewish doctrine, time is divided into two ages or *æons*, the age present, and the age to come. The "last day" is the end of the present age and ushers in the new. Like the other Apostles, S. John expects this consummation in the near future. In his Epistle he writes, "it is the last hour" I. 2 18. This is not the same as the last day; it means rather the hour preceding the day; for it is marked by the signs which were to precede the consummation, and the coming of Christ, namely, by the appearance of the antichrist I. 2 18-22. S. John speaks of many antichrists, and displays here his disposition to see the fulfilment of prophecy in the events transacting about him; but there is in this no essential contradiction to the prophetic tradition of a single antichrist, for the spirit of the "many false prophets" is one, and as "the spirit of error" it is contrasted with "the Spirit of truth" I. 4 6.

The belief in a final day of judgment is thus incontestably clear in S. John's writings *cf.* Rev. 20 12 13. Far less clear is the nature of the punishment which is meted out to the unbelieving world. S. John, whose interest is engrossed with the positive accomplishment of salvation, does not dwell with predilection upon the reverse of the picture. It is in general sufficient to know that the world is judged; this judgment is however further expressed by the fact that "the prince of this world shall be cast out" 12 31 *cf.* 16 11. Christ has "overcome the world" 16 33, and S. John as he writes his Epistle sees the world as a power which is indeed still able to persecute and tempt the Church, but which the Church can overcome through the superior might of Christ 4 4, and which already " is passing away with its lusts " 2 17. In his parable of the vine Jesus says, " If a man abide not in me, he is cast forth as a branch, and is withered; and they gather them, and cast them into the fire, and they are burned " 15 6. The very phraseology of this verse recalls the saying, likewise parabolic, of Mat. 13 40, according to which the gathering and burning of the tares occurs " in the consummation of the age." Both the Jewish and the Christian view of the last judgment represented it as a partition of life and death, and " the resurrection of judgment " which S. John contrasts with " the resurrection of life " 5 29 would seem to indicate the same conception. As eternal life was the specific gift which Christ brings to the world, we can hardly conceive that the punishment of the wicked could consist in anything but the deprivation of this gift, namely, in abandonment to death. This would seem to accord peculiarly well with the characteristics of S. John's thought. The "sin unto death" of which S. John speaks in his Epistle 5 16, refers primarily to the Jewish discrimination between sins, the legal penalty of which was death, and such as admitted of ritual atonement: but doubtless S. John thought of the eternal death which is God's final punishment for sin; — *cf.* Rev. 21 8 " the second death." As the immunity of believers from judgment is founded upon the fact that they have already " passed out of death into life," so the doom of him that loveth not is simply expressed as an *abiding in death* I. 3 14.

The condemnation of the world, so far as it concerns the positive completion of salvation, is satisfied in this, that every evil thing opposed to God is abolished.

4. The Election of the Children of God

God's Election

We have seen that the division which is brought about by Christ's appearance among men results, on the one hand, in the dissolution of the previous covenant relation of the Jews by their own rejection of the Messiah; and on the other, in the establishment of a new family of God's children upon the ground of their believing reception of him. The company which is thus gathered together, separated from the world, and drawn to God, by their loving reception of the light, is nothing less than a new covenant congregation which steps into the place vacated by the old. They also are Jesus' "own" (*cf.* 1 11 with 13 1); and being his, they are the Father's possession and the people of God 10 14 26 29 17 9 10. But no people can by its own choice become God's possession: it is only by God's free grace that men are called into his fellowship. It was a maxim in Israel that God had not chosen the nation on account of its superior excellence or might, but because he loved his people. It was no otherwise in the new covenant relation: it was Jesus' choice and not their own which constituted the disciples his possession 15 16 19; and in the last resort it was God himself who separated them from the world and brought them to Jesus 17 6; they were his because they were already his Father's and were given unto him 6 37 39 10 29 17 2. This time however God's election was not a national but an individual one. It was indifferent to the question of race 1 13; the Jews themselves were accorded no privilege above other peoples, but as many of them as were truly Christ's sheep were " put forth " of the Jewish fold ($\dot{\epsilon}\kappa\beta\acute{a}\lambda\eta$ 10 4 *cf.* 9 34), in order that they, as well as the children of God who were scattered throughout the world, might be gathered together as one flock under one shepherd 10 16 11 52.

Notwithstanding the individuality of God's choice, S. John emphasises highly the unity of the flock; and although God's people are thus gathered from out all the world, they are even more thoroughly sundered from the world, more radically contrasted with the world, than were the covenant race of old.

The Covenant People This we have briefly discussed under another topic, pp. 130 *seq.* Because they are not of it, God's people must expect the world's hatred 15 20; while they are in the world they must endure persecution, but they may nevertheless " be of good cheer," for Jesus has " overcome the world " 16 33; — or, as S. John says in his Epistle, " greater is he that is in you than he that is in the world " I. 4 4.

This separation of the people of God from the world is not a nominal, but a real one: they are not only *called* the children of God, but such they *are* I. 3 1. They are "*in truth*" what the people of the Old Covenant were in a figure. The Christian is God's child because he is actually begotten of God. This relation manifests itself by ethical likeness to God I. 2 29 3 9 4 7, which in heaven will be perfected I. 3 2, and which on earth constitutes a family in which brotherly love, as among actual brothers, is perfectly spontaneous and natural I. 5 ¹ ². Israel was called God's vine, Ps. 80 Jer. 2 ²¹ Hos. 10 ¹; but Christ is "the true vine" and his disciples are the branches 15 ¹ *seq.* In contrast to the Jews — whose worship was nevertheless an intelligent one 4 ²² — the Christians are "the true worshippers," and "worship the Father in spirit and in truth" 4 ²³. Instead of the figurative Temple, Jesus' body is the true Temple 2 ²¹, because it more really represents God's presence among men. The essential importance of the Temple is that it represents God's abiding presence among his people. In the Christian community, as in the heavenly Jerusalem, Rev. 21 ²², there is no temple needed, "for God himself and the Lamb are the Temple thereof." Even when Jesus has ascended to heaven, it is still true that God is in the midst of his people I. 4 ⁴; and the idea of the Temple is completely fulfilled in the mystical union of the believer with God, in his taking up his abode within each disciple 14 ²³, of which we are assured "by the Spirit which he gave us" I. 3 ²⁴ 4 ¹³.

The people of God, who in reality do not belong to the world, are sent into the world, even as Christ was sent into the world 17 ¹⁸; and for the purpose of this mission they must be sanctified "in truth," as Christ sanctified himself 17 ¹⁹. They are to be a holy people, as Israel was of old, set apart and consecrated to the Lord. This sanctification is wrought by God 17 ¹⁷, and by Christ 17 ¹⁹; but it requires also on the part of the believer continuous ethical effort to preserve himself from all contamination of the world I. 3 ³ *cf.* 15 ². Christians are engaged in an ethical struggle with the world. They must keep themselves pure, not only from idolatry, but from every such relation to the world, and to the things which are in the world, as would prove essential community with it. They may not love the world, nor the specious pleasures which it offers, "for all that is in the world, the lust of the flesh, the lust of the eyes, and the vainglory of life, is not of the Father, but is of the world. And the world passeth away, and the lust thereof" I. 2 16 17. The result of this struggle is not doubtful, for in the last resort it is God's might and not man's which gains the victory. Christ has overcome the world, and his victory is the ground of the disciples' confidence 16 33. The victory of the children of God over the world is grounded in the fact, that "greater is he that is in you than he that is in the world" I. 4 4. "We know that whosoever is begotten of God sinneth not; but he that was begotten of God keepeth him, and the Evil One toucheth him not" I. 5 18. It is clear from this last verse that S. John cannot think of the possibility of a true member of the family of God falling away into apostasy. The more decidedly man's relation to God is traced back to God's own choice and work, so much the more difficult is it to think of the continuance of this relationship as dependent upon human fickleness. The very fact however of the extension of the Christian community in the world, brings with it the possibility that heterogeneous elements may mix with it. Deceivers I. 2 4 and deceived I. 1 8, Christians only "in tongue" I. 3 18, even children of the Devil I. 3 10, false teachers and lying prophets, can for a time appear as members of the community, although they are of the world, and finally return to the world where they belong and where they find a hearing I. 4 5. The community, like the individual, must continually purify itself from the contamination of the world; and S. John sees in the severing of these false members from the Church, the proof "that they all are not of us" I. 2 19.

But not only is the final victory assured for the children of God; they are altogether kept from sin. Upon this point S. John's statements are clear and emphatic enough, but they seem to be involved in a radical contradiction. On the one hand he says: "Whosoever is begotten of God doeth no sin, because his seed abideth in him, and he cannot sin, because he is begotten of God" I. 3 9. It is only in appearance that this contradicts I. 1 7-10, for this is in a sense the continuation of the Baptist's preaching of repentance, and may perhaps be referred especially to sins committed before the cleansing by the blood of Jesus, which is received upon entrance into the Christian community, and he goes on to warn those who have become Christians against sin. This requires him however either to leave quite hopeless the brother who does nevertheless commit sin; and with his absolute, "He that sinneth hath not seen him, neither knoweth him," to cut him off from any communion with God; or to point out to him some still remaining possibility of forgiveness. This latter he does by pointing to Jesus and his priestly intercession with God I. 2 1. Jesus' sacrifice was made once and for all I. 2 2, but his priesthood is perpetual and eternal. The contradiction which is here involved in S. John's expression, is only partly resolved by distinguishing between sin as a habit, and particular acts of sin (see page 110), for S. John's language does not consistently observe this discrimination. For S. John, as for the Jews, sin is transgression of law ($\dot{a}\nu o\mu i a$) I. 3 4. The Old Covenant discriminated between sins of ignorance, for which pardon might be had through ritual atonement, Num. 15 27, and sins done "with a high hand," which involved irrevocable separation from the Covenant, Num. 15 30 31. So also S. John distinguishes between the wilful (*cf.* Heb. 10 26) breach of God's Covenant, which irretrievably forfeits that eternal life which is to be had only in the Christian brotherhood, and sins for which a brother's intercession may still avail to obtain restoration to communion in the brotherhood, and to participation in life I. 5 16. The distinction is however not quite the same in the two cases, for the Christian Law is no longer expressed in external ordinances, which a man might in ignorance transgress; but in the single principle of likeness to God, of love; therefore as so inward an affair that it is at bottom impossible to conceive of any transgression of it which is not a presumptuous breach of covenant, a manifestation of radical subjection to the darkness and to the dominion of the Devil, to whom all hatred is traced. But sin is a broader conception than this: "all unrighteousness ($\dot{a}\delta\iota\kappa i a$) is sin" I. 5 17; every instance of yielding to the temptations of the world, of straying from the way of absolute rectitude, although it does not involve a radical deflection of the heart from God, is sin; — "and there is sin not unto death." This is explained symbolically in the Gospel, by Jesus' washing of the disciples' feet: "He that is bathed needeth not save to wash his feet, but is clean every whit" 13 10. The lustration of the New Covenant cleanses perfectly and for ever, there is needed no second bath, but only a washing of the feet from such contamination as is inevitable to all who walk in the world.

There is one instance in which even the necessity of confession and forgiveness for the Christian is quite left out of account. In I. 3 $^{18\text{-}20}$ it is said: "Children, let us not love in word, neither with the tongue; but in deed and truth. Hereby shall we know that we are of the truth, and shall assure our heart before him, whereinsoever our heart condemn us; because God is greater than our heart, and knoweth all things." In the consciousness of fulfilling God's commandment by a genuine love of the brethren, the Christian need not be for ever perturbed by his own conscience convicting him of particular delinquencies, for God who knoweth all judgeth according to the inmost disposition of the heart. It was in this thought S. Peter found relief, when after his fall Jesus examines him: "Lovest thou me?" — His own heart testified against him, accusing him of denial; but in the assurance of true love, he appeals to the superior knowledge of him who knows all: "Lord, thou knowest all things; thou knowest that I love thee" 21 $^{15\text{-}17}$.

We have seen in the foregoing how readily S. John applies to the Christian community, the ideas of covenant relationship which were familiar to the Jews. It is therefore a ground for some surprise that he does not use the word covenant, nor expressly contrast the Christian community with the Jewish. This seems to indicate that, although he felt for himself a personal necessity of constructing his theology in the terms of Hebrew thought, he did not find in the idea of the Covenant the highest expression of the salvation brought by Christ; and that in this instance, as in so many others, he avoided the use of words which were alien to his gentile readers.

How unserviceable this word was for the expression of the idea of salvation to native heathen, we can see from the devices by which S. Paul, Gal. 3 15, and the author of Hebrews 9 16 *seq.* sought to adopt it to their modes of thought.

It is a ground of far more surprise that he also omits the name which designated Christ's disciples, in their organised unity, as the people of God. The word *Church* (ἐκκλησία) occurs only in the third Epistle, and then only in relation to the individual congregation III. 6 9 10. There was of course no reason for its use in the Gospel, and its omission in the Epistle may be an accident. At any rate no one could lay more emphasis than does S. John upon the conceptions which were most fundamental to the Christian idea of the Church; in particular upon the unity of the whole brotherhood, the very idea which the name Church in its universal reference was meant to express. The pre-eminence of the Apostles is also clearly recognised 13 20 15 16 17 18 20 21 I. 1 3 4 6 II. 10 III. 9 *seq.*, and it is recorded in 20 23 how Christ bestowed upon them plenipotentiary authority; though their unique function in the Church is more commonly referred to the fact that they are true witnesses of the historical manifestation of Jesus, having been with him from the beginning 15 27 19 35 I. 1 1-5. As however it is God's power which protects the disciple from evil, and as direct fellowship with him is the highest Christian ideal; so too it is the distinction of the people of the New Covenant as the prophet foretold, Jer. 31 ^{34}, that "they shall be all taught of God" 6 ^{45}. It is no longer necessary for every man to teach his brother, for the Holy Spirit directly teaches them all things 14 ^{26}. In the same way it is said in the Epistle: "Ye have an anointing from the Holy One, and ye know all things" 2 ^{20}. Even the Apostolic teaching is not indispensable to God's children who are thus gifted with prophetic inspiration of the truth: "And as for you, the anointing which ye received of him abideth in you, and ye need not that any one teach you; but as his anointing teacheth you concerning all things, and is true, and is no lie, and even as it taught you, ye abide in him" I. 2 ^{27}.

We have in this chapter already studied a number of the traits which mark the Christian community as God's covenant people; but we have still to note the most important element of the Covenant. If a company of sinful men gathered out of the world was to be brought into real communion with God; it could be accomplished only by doing away with that which on the part of men constituted an absolute impediment to such communion: with all impurity, and above all with sin. This obvious condition determined the conception of the foundation of the Old The Sacrifice and Lustration of the New Covenant Covenant; and the New also could not even be thought of apart from the ideas of purification and expiation. It is the more necessary to emphasise this point because it is frequently asserted that the idea of atonement has absolutely no place in S. John's writings, and that Christ's death has importance only as a manifestation of his love. Some even of those who admit S. John's authorship of the Epistle, contend that his emphatic representations of Christ's death in the aspect of a sacrifice, are merely echoes of conceptions elsewhere current in the Church, and have no organic place in S. John's theology. But the Gospel too furnishes very distinct expressions of the objective significance of Christ's death; and although it is unquestionably true that the idea of atonement does not — as with S. Paul and the author of Hebrews — occupy the foremost place in his representation; that indeed it recedes before the predominant representation of the moral effectiveness of Christ's revelation; it nevertheless remains the *sine qua non* of fellowship with God. Jesus is not only Truth, Light, and Life; he is also " the propitiation for our sins " I. 2 $_2$. In I. 4 $_{10}$ this is actually represented as God's purpose in sending the Son. And when in the preceding and parallel verse, God's purpose is defined in different terms — " in order that we might live through him " — it is clear that the author thinks of men as fallen into a state of death through their sin, and saved from this judgment by Christ's sin-offering. With this hint we see the significance of such words as 6 $_{51}$, that Jesus' flesh offered in death will give life to the world. The world is in a state of death on account of sin, and therefore in need of salvation, which in such a case cannot be thought of apart from atonement 3 $_{17}$ 4 $_{42}$ 12 $_{47}$ I. 4 $_{14}$. And if we have a right to interpret I. 4 $_9$, according to the following verse, we cannot read the similar saying in the Gospel 3 $_{16}$, without a reference to Jesus' death. At any rate there is a reference to Jesus' death in verse 14 of the same chapter, if we may interpret it as S. John does the similar saying 12 33.

The significance of Jesus' death is thought of more particularly with reference to the very foundation of the New Covenant congregation. It is not only the shepherd's voice which gathers together the scattered sheep and constitutes them one flock 10 16; the laying down of his life is also necessary to this end 10 11 15 17. And although Jesus' death cannot according to the terms of the parable be represented in a sacrificial aspect; the thought is expressed that it avails not only to save the life of the sheep from the wolf's attack 10 12, but to give them a more abundant life 10 10. How important this conception was for S. John himself, we see in 11 50-52: "It is expedient for you that one man should die for the people, and that the whole Nation perish not. Now this he said not of himself: but being high priest that year, he prophesied that Jesus should die for the Nation; and not for the Nation only, but that he might gather into one the children of God that are scattered abroad." He here interprets Caiaphas' astute counsel as a prophecy of Jesus' death as a sacrifice for the Nation, and more particularly as the covenant sacrifice which constituted the scattered children of God one people. It is likewise S. John's own interpretation of Jesus' words, which represents his death as the event which draws all men unto him 12 32 33. In 17 19 Jesus represents himself more expressly as the covenant sacrifice which consecrates his disciples as God's people: "For their sakes I consecrate myself, that they themselves also may be consecrated in truth." In view of the fact that Jesus has already entered upon the way to his death, this saying can only refer to his sacrificial consecration to God; and the consecration of his disciples, which he thereby effects, is a consecration to God's possession as a covenant people (*cf.* Heb. 2 11 10 10 13 12). This is a consecration " in truth," because it in reality accomplishes that which the Old Covenant sacrifices of beasts represented only in a figure. Jesus' death as a covenant sacrifice has reference solely to the covenant people. Although we have seen that his saving work, and in particular his "propitiation," is "*for*" the whole world I. 2 2; it is effectual only for those who stand within the covenant congregation. The Old Testament idea of the Covenant was essentially that of peculiar and exclusive privilege: the New Covenant was likewise exclusive, though only those were excluded who were self-excluded. The forgiveness of sins was one of the privileges of the Old Covenant, and it was prophetically promised as one of the special blessings of the New. It is therefore thoroughly in accord with the Old Testament view when S. John represents that only he who by walking in the light has come into fellowship with God, and stands thereby in fellowship with God's people, can enjoy the cleansing of his sins through Christ's blood I. 1 7. The same conception is postulated in the use of the Old Testament phrase, "faithful and just" ($\pi\iota\sigma\tau\acute{o}\varsigma$ $\kappa\alpha\grave{\iota}$ $\delta\acute{\iota}\kappa\alpha\iota o\varsigma$) I. 1 9. It is only in relation to the Covenant that God's mercy in forgiving sins can be characterised as an act of faithfulness and justice; but where the covenant atonement is already provided, and the confession of sins is truly made, forgiveness is simply a consequence of God's faithfulness to his promise and his righteousness in observing the covenanted terms.

Christ's sacrifice, like the sacrifice of the Covenant in Ex. 24, was made once for all. Moreover, in the Christian dispensation there was no provision of repeated sacrifices for recurrent sins; for the purpose of Christ's coming was, both by his sacrifice I 29, and by his total manifestation I. 3 5, "to take away sins;" and we have already seen that for God's children, sin and the sinful power is already radically overcome and abolished.

It would indeed be strange if the sacrificial idea were ignored in a Gospel which begins with the Baptist's witness to the lamb of God I 29, and ends by representing Jesus' death as occurring on the very day, perhaps at the very hour, when the Passover was wont to be slain. It was Jesus himself who represented his death as a covenant sacrifice of atonement when at the Last Supper he took the cup, and said: "This is my blood of the Covenant." The phrase is clearly a reproduction of Ex. 24 8, *cf.* Heb. 9 20. S. Mark 14 24 adds, "which is shed for many;" and S. Matthew 26 28, still further, "for the remission of sins." S. Paul I. Cor. 11 25, and S. Luke 22 20, unite in calling it the cup of "the *New* Covenant in my blood;" and this conception was firmly rooted in the Church. We cannot point to any single sacrifice of the Old Testament cultus as the exclusive type of Christ's sacrifice: it fulfilled the idea of sacrifice in general. It was in particular the foundation of a covenant; but many of the sacrifices recorded in the Old Testament besides that of Ex. 24 were of this character. The Passover, Ex. 13, was a covenant sacrifice of earlier date, and more primitive type; and many of its inspiring ideas have survived in the Christian Eucharist. It represented not only a national, but a family covenant, and like every covenant sacrifice its benefits were shared only by those who ate it. It was also more closely a type of Christ's sacrifice, because of its particular reference to deliverance from death. S. John does not record the institution of the Christian Passover: it was sufficiently well known through the earlier Gospels, and through the common practice of the Church. But Jesus' discourse in chapter 6 $_{51-58}$ is an indubitable reference to it: his hard saying could not have been completely intelligible till after his sacrificial death. We have already observed how in this chapter S. John blends the subjective and objective points of view: in verse 40 it is "he that beholdeth the Son, and believeth on him has eternal life;" whereas in verse 54 it is "he that eateth my flesh and drinketh my blood." But this does not render less real the reference to Jesus' objective sacrifice; it is rather this element which is the ultimate explanation of the life-giving effect of his manifestation. Here too it is the eating of the sacrificial flesh which conditions communion with Christ 6 $_{56}$, the gift of eternal life 6 $_{53\ 58}$, and resurrection from the dead 6 $_{54}$, or escape from death 6 $_{50}$. It is true that the idea of sacrifice is not only blended with other conceptions, but altogether raised from the plane of merely ritual and legal conception, to the loftiest mysticism; but it shows nevertheless how fundamental was the notion of sacrifice in S. John's estimation of Christ's work.

We have still to speak of the lustrations of the

New Covenant. Ritual lustrations were a special feature of the old dispensation, and a general cleansing with water was particularly prophesied as a preparation for the coming of the Messiah, Ez. 36 25. S. John lays very special emphasis upon the Baptist's mission, as the preparation for the Messiah; and although he does not expressly consider the character and necessity of S. John's baptism, he had the less reason to do so because it survived in the Christian practice, and was therefore a matter of universal acquaintance. He does not however disparage S. John's baptism with water, by contrasting it with the spiritual baptism of the Messiah 1 26 31 33; for the same form was continued by Christ and his disciples 3 22, 4 1. Jesus closely associated himself with the Baptist 3 11 when he spoke to Nicodemus about the ethical cleansing which was necessary for entrance into the kingdom of God 3 3 5. This baptism was indeed one of the Spirit, as well as of water; but Jesus nevertheless classes this ethical purification amongst the earthly things which a teacher of Israel might be supposed to understand, and which he himself had witnessed as the fruit of the Baptist's mission 3 10-12. Necessary as it was, however, the cleansing with water did not involve the forgiveness of sins, which was possible only on the ground of Christ's sacrifice. This difference between Christ's purification and that of the Baptist, S. John suggests in the Epistle 5 6-9. Christ came, not like the Baptist "with the water only," "but with the water and with the blood;" and this serves as his witness that he is the one to whose coming the Scripture testifies. For although the Scripture testifies that the Messianic era must begin with a cleansing with water, Ez. 36 25, it is not therefore the bringer of the water who is " he that cometh," for the Scripture also testifies to a general remission of sins on the ground of a sin offering, which Jesus made in his blood. This explains the interest with which S. John notes the mingling of water and blood from Jesus' pierced side 19 34 35. Blood I. 1 9, as well as water, is a purifying agent, and we are almost compelled to suppose that S. John had in mind Zechariah's prophecy of the " fountain opened for sin and for uncleanness " 13 1, which follows almost immediately after the phrase which he quotes in this connection, " they shall look on him whom they pierced " 19 37 Zech. 12 10. We see now the importance of the triple testimony which he adduces in the Epistle 5 7-9. It was to Isaiah's prophecy, particularly to chapter 53 (*cf.* 59 21), that the Baptist himself implicitly referred 1 29, to express the contrast between his own mission and that of the Messiah. The Messiah must come not with baptism alone, but with the blood of atonement, and with the gift of the Spirit. It is thus that Jesus came: with the water of baptism and the blood of atonement he brings also the gift of the Spirit 7 37-39; — therefore, "the Spirit beareth witness, because the Spirit is the truth" I. 5 7, and all three, the Spirit, the water, and the blood, agree in one witness, which is the witness of God concerning his Son I. 5 8 9, as the Messiah who comes in fulfilment of prophecy.

B. REALISATION OF THE POSITIVE CONCEPT OF SALVATION THROUGH THE REVELATION OF THE TRUTH

Under the general topic of this chapter, The Life Manifested, we have thus far considered what is involved in the very fact of the coming of the Logos into the world and his becoming flesh: the judicial discrimination which is effected amongst men by his manifestation in the world; the consequent doom of the world, and the election out of the world of a covenant people, who through Christ's death enjoy forgiveness and cleansing from sin, and access to God. These considerations have to do predominantly, though not exclusively (for we would not sharply draw a distinction where S. John does not draw it), with the objective aspects of salvation. But we have already remarked that the preponderating emphasis of S. John's representation lies rather upon the subjective appropriation of salvation, which also is the more positive conception, because it deals not with what man is saved from, but with what he is saved to; with the positive realisation of salvation in the children of God, rather than with its mere conditions. Eternal life is the key-note of this section, and with it we consider the whole range of ideas with which it is most characteristically associated. Of these, the first is the truth, which Christ himself revealed, and after him and in his stead the Spirit. The truth, or the light, being appropriated by faith, issues in the knowledge of God, which at once produces life in men, and constitutes an essential element of it; — an essential element, but not the whole of the idea of life; for fellowship in its triple form (with Christ, with the Father and with the brethren), which is as we have seen brought about by the death of Christ, and yet in this connection seems to be more directly conditioned by the believing reception of the light, is the chief element of S. John's idea of life, and the very fulness of Christian joy. This divine life in God's children is both manifested and tested by filial likeness to the Father. Christian ethics is from this point of view the spontaneous fruit of the true life; although it is also directly conditioned by a true knowledge of God, and displayed by imitation of him; — pre-eminently by love. It is, as we might expect, in the Epistle rather than in the Gospel that we find the clearest and most developed expression of S. John's own thought. We have seen that S. John derived his doctrine not only from Jesus' express teaching, but from meditation upon his manifestation as a whole; and though this is peculiarly true of his estimate of the significance of Jesus' Person, it is likewise true of his conception of the boon which he bestowed upon the world; — of that eternal life which is appropriate to the Christian community, its nature, its genesis, and the forms of its manifestation. This is not to deny what we have already repeatedly noticed, that almost all of S. John's characteristic ideas occur also in Christ's speeches; and in general we may say that no idea emerges in the Epistle which has not its text in the Gospel. But it is perfectly in accordance with the nature of the case that the Epistle, which is the normal expression of S. John's religious consciousness, presents his own theological conceptions more prominently. The ideas which we have to consider in this section — the Spirit and the truth, faith and the knowledge of God, the new birth and eternal life, the Christian fellowship and likeness to God — are all of them common in the New Testament, and yet each is in itself and in its associations in greater or less degree peculiar to S. John. We have however to guard against two misconceptions at this point. In the first place we must not regard this scheme of thought as though it were a system complete in itself and independent of the more objective considerations we have just been studying; for, though we have here isolated it for the sake of clearness of treatment, it is not thus discriminated by S. John, but is, as we have seen, associated so closely with the purely objective significance of Christ's work, that the same fact is at the same time regarded from both points of view (see page 30 *seq.*). In the second place, we must not exaggerate the independence of S. John's thought in this particular; for even this most characteristic sequence of thought has its root in the Old Testament. The Son of God, by his essential likeness to the Father, revealed God to men, and so placed them in that true communion with him which is the very fruition of eternal life. This is the briefest expression of S. John's Gospel. There is no single passage which so completely sums up this message as the penultimate verse of the Epistle, "*We know that the Son of God is come, and hath given us an understanding, that we know* (διάνοιαν ἵνα γινώσκωμεν) *him that is true, and are in him that is true, in his Son Jesus Christ.* This *is the True God and eternal life."* This saying is however in its most significant part the reproduction of an Old Testament promise; — " I will give them a heart to know me, that I am the LORD" Jer. 24 7. In the same verse, the consequence of God's disclosure of himself in the very hearts of men is expressed in this, that " they shall be my people, and I will be their God." This mutual approach and appropriation on the part of God and his people is virtually a new covenant which rests upon a new and intimate knowledge of God. And another passage which is in many respects parallel, Jer. 31 31-34, promises expressly the establishment of a new covenant, in place of the one which had been broken, upon the basis of forgiveness of sins, and of such a knowledge of God as should make his law an inward revelation, written upon the heart.

In the very nature of the case, a positive relation of men to God can come about only by his revelation of himself. It was God's revelation of himself on Sinai which, more positively than the sacrifices there inaugurated, brought Israel into covenant relation to God; and God's covenants with the Patriarchs rested upon a new revelation of his Name, Gen. 32 29 Ex. 6 3. According to the Hebrew idea, a name ought to be descriptive of the essence of the object named; and it is on this account that the Name by which God reveals himself is a matter of such profound significance. S. John retains this pregnant Hebraism, recording Jesus' profession of the accomplishment of his mission, "I manifested thy Name unto the men whom thou gavest me out of the world" 17 6; and his prayer, " Holy Father, keep them in thy Name" 17 11. The Name by which God has made himself known to the Church, is most adequately expressed by S. Paul: "The God and Father of our Lord Jesus Christ" Eph. 1 3 Col. 1 3 II. Cor. 1 1 31; and S. John's idea is substantially the same when he records that unique saying in which Jesus made over to his disciples the conception of the divine paternity which he had hitherto so highly exalted by appropriating it to himself: "My Father and your Father, and my God and your God" 20 17.

Old Testament prophecy was at one in the expectation that the Messianic time would be distinguished by a more profound and more general knowledge of God Is. 11 9 59 21 Joel 3 1 *seq.*, so that all being taught of God, would need no human teachers, Jer. 31 34; and that there would be wrought therewith a radical moral change in the Nation Is. 1 27 29 23 32 1 *seq.* 15 *seq.* 33 5 Ez. 11 19 36 25 *seq.* Zeph. 3 12. But the prophetic pictures differed very distinctly in respect to the instrumentality by which this new revelation was to be brought about. Jeremiah thought rather of a quickening and deepening of the religious consciousness, which did not require an actual manifestation of God; other prophets however expect such a revelation of the divine glory as shall surpass even the manifestation upon Sinai, Is. 40 5. The inauguration of the era of salvation will unquestionably be God's own work; but, as in the establishment of the Old Covenant, this may be accomplished through chosen instruments; and therefore it is a prophet that is expected, Deut. 18 15 18, or especially the Messianic King who shall realise God's will upon earth by the establishment of God's kingdom, Jer. 33 15 21. The diversity of the prophetic pictures of the coming age, explains the variety in the Messianic expectation which Jesus encountered among the Jews. It furnished also a problem for Christian theology to solve. For from the beginning the Church was confident of possessing in Jesus all that God had promised his people; and it had therefore to show how the diverse lines of prophecy terminated in him. It is S. John's distinction to have solved this problem more perfectly than any other writer in the New Testament. He represented Jesus not only as Prophet and as King, but as God; — the Word of God become flesh, manifesting the divine glory in his own person, and thus imparting the vision of God to men. The advance which S. John makes from the revelation which Jesus was able to impart by reason of his perfect knowledge of God, to the revelation which was given in his work and in his nature, the vision of God in the Person of Jesus; is — although it is not without analogy in other parts of the New Testament — the most characteristic and the most precious contribution which he has made to Christian theology. The preponderance of this idea in S. John's writings, his representation of the saving potency of the revelation of God in Christ, which of itself regenerates, sanctifies, produces eternal life, establishes fellowship with God and amongst the brethren, and conditions the Christian morality; is so far from being a strange departure from the Old Testament type of thought, that it is rather, beyond any other representation of the New Testament, the most faithful to the prophecy of the Messianic age, which likewise pictured salvation predominantly in terms of the revelation and knowledge of God.

The New Birth — The Light of Life

We have already studied the significance of S. John's definition, " God is light; " we have seen that God is also the source of life, and that the Logos who *Christ the Truth* was of like nature was therefore the light of the world, the life which he shared with the Father becoming the light of men. Keeping in mind these fundamental conceptions, we have here merely to consider how this divine life is imparted to God's children; how the truth — that is the revelation of God through Jesus' word and work — being appropriated by faith, issues in that knowledge of God which is the condition of eternal life.

In the first place we have to consider the relation of Christ himself to this impartation of life through the truth. We have only to rehearse at this point what has been more fully stated in another place (especially page 86 *seq.*). We have seen how S. John's whole theology turns on this point; how his choice of the name Logos was itself conditioned by the desire to represent Jesus as the personal revelation of God; how Jesus is the *Way* to *life* just because he is the *Truth* 14 6; how his revelation is the light which conditions life 8 12. Jesus himself represents his mission in the world as essentially a "witness," a recounting of the "heavenly things" which he had seen with the Father 3 11 12; and it is his "interpretation" of the invisible 1 18, his "message" concerning the nature of God I. 1 5, which is for the Evangelist the chief end of his manifestation. Among the so-called offices of Christ, it is that of Prophet which is pre-eminent in

S. John's representation. Jesus' claim to be King rests upon the fact that he bears witness to the truth, and this is in fact the very end and aim of his birth and mission in the world 18 37. It is S. John especially who gives us information about the popular estimation of Jesus as a prophet 1 21 25 6 14 7 40. The Baptist witnesses to him as to a prophet: "He whom God hath sent" — the ambassador of God *par excellence* — who "speaketh the words of God," and like every prophet is furnished with God's Spirit, but unlike any other prophet, "not by measure" 3 34. It is his prophetic function which Jesus makes prominent when he says, "The words which thou hast given unto me, I have given unto them" 17 8; when he represents himself as "sent," particularly in the saying, "The Father which sent me, he has given me a commandment what I should speak" 12 49. Jesus speaks of himself as a prophet 4 44, and associates himself closely with the Baptist 3 11. He describes himself as "a man that hath told you the truth, which I heard from God" 8 40. It is thus that S. John carries out in his historical representation the general conception of Christ as the revealing Word and the light of the world.

Jesus is the medium of life to the world 10 28 17 2 I. 4 9 5 11 12. We have seen that this is along one line of thought particularly referred to his sacrificial death; along the line which we are at present pursuing, it is referred to the fact that he is the revelation of God. He is the medium of life, because he is the "Word of life" I. 1 1. He is the life manifested I. 1 2, and the revelation of the divine nature which in him has been brought within the apprehension of human faculties — heard, seen, beheld, handled — is the foundation of the Christian fellowship I. 1 3, and the ground of Christian joy I. 1 4. But it is not only the total manifestation of God in the Word, nor the expression of the divine nature as light; which is life-giving 8 12, and conditions Christian fellowship; Jesus' several sayings, his words, are also life-giving (ῥήματα) 6 63 69; his commandment is eternal life 12 50; and abiding in his word, or keeping it, insures deliverance from death 8 51, is the condition of true discipleship 8 31, and of fellowship with God 14 23. So also in chapter 10, it is Jesus' voice which draws together the scattered sheep into one flock 10 3 16 27. Jesus' word has also the power to cleanse 15 3, and this power — as indeed every other which is ascribed to it — is due to the fact that it is in reality the Father's word, and that it is the truth 17 17. It is the truth which sanctifies, and which makes free 8 32. Walking or abiding in the truth I. 3 19 II. 4 III. 3 4, is the same as walking or abiding in the light I. 1 7 2 10.

The knowledge of God is the condition of eternal life; and this is what is meant in 17 3: "This is eternal life, that they should know thee the only true God, and him whom thou didst send, Jesus Christ." This was not a notion strange to the Jews, for they themselves thought to possess eternal life in the revelation of their Scriptures (an idea which has many points of contact in the Old Testament, Deut. 32 47, particularly in the wisdom literature, see Ps. 119 50 93); and Christ's assertion was to the effect that *his* revelation, as the only adequate one, could alone give life.

S. John's representation reaches its highest expression in 6 40, " that every one that beholdeth the

Son, and believeth on him, should have eternal life" *cf.* 12 45; —just as in the case of the serpent, Num. 21 8 (see 3 14): He that looketh shall live.

We have hitherto considered the vision of God only as it was manifested by Jesus' bodily presence upon earth. But the same Gospel whose earlier part treats of the coming of the light into the world 1 9 3 19 12 35 46, treats at the end of Jesus' departure out of the world 13 1. It would be a poor fulfilment of the prophecy which promised an enduring covenant, and an eternal presence of God among his people, if with Jesus' ascension the newly given vision came to an end, and remoteness succeeded again to the close relation of fellowship with God which Jesus had established. Jesus' departure from the world was in fact a turning-point of the highest importance. The sensible, visible manifestation of God before all the world came thereby to an end. That Jesus was the light of the world as long as he was in the world 9 5, signifies that for the world at least his departure was the disappearance of the light and the closing in of darkness 12 35 36. Hence it is said, "the life *was* the light of men," and "he *was* in the world" 1 4 10. Jesus' separation from the world signified therefore a judgment upon it 12 31 16 10. Because the world has neither recognised nor received God's revelation 17 25 1. 3 1 it falls back into the dominion of the darkness 12 35. The illumination which is experienced in Christ is however an enduring one for those who by faithful reception of the light have broken the bonds of the darkness 12 46 8 12, and become sons of light 12 36. For them the

The Spirit of Truth

true light continues to shine I. 2 8; they are in the light I. 2 9, and "walk in the light, as he is in the light" I. 1 7; and so is fulfilled in them the promise made concerning Jerusalem: "The LORD shall be thy everlasting light" Is. 60 20.

Jesus' departure out of the world had moreover the effect of revealing him more clearly as the Son of man who was from heaven 3 13, and of removing the causes of stumbling which were due to an imperfect recognition of his nature 6 61 62. But above everything else, the "lifting up" of the Son of man 3 14, serves to make him accessible to the faith of all 3 15. S. John is perfectly well aware of the double meaning of this expression. He finds in it indeed a hint of the mode of Jesus' death 12 33 18 32, and so derives from Jesus' own words a proof of the significance of his death. He also sees in it a revelation of Jesus' veritable character and dignity 8 28, and of his love and obedience to the Father 14 31. But above all it denotes, according to its primary meaning, his transcendence of earthly limitation and elevation to heaven, whence he can exercise universal rule, and make his saving work effectual for *all* 12 32. The departure from this world which is accomplished in his death, is therefore anything rather than a breaking off of his relation with the world. Only as the one who gives his life, in order that he may take it again 10 17 12 24, does Jesus attain to the universal significance which his mission demands 10 16 11 52. Jesus' revealing work not only continues, but in becoming more spiritual, more immediate and more inward, it is able to lay aside the restrictions which clung to his earthly teaching 16 25. It is precisely as he is exalted to heaven that Jesus is able to come into the most inward and direct relation with his disciples;—" I in them and they in me."

The conception of Jesus' continued influence upon and presence among his disciples, is founded upon the idea of his " coming again," which S. John distinguishes, as well from his visible reappearance after his resurrection, 16 16 *seq.* as from his final return 14 3. Jesus will not leave his disciples orphaned, he will come, and though hidden from the world he remains for *them* an enduring vision. His unity with the Father constitutes the ground of the disciples' fellowship with God. It is no longer *I*, but " *We* will come and make our abode with him " 14 18 23.

This coming again of Jesus, and abiding forever with his disciples, is explicitly referred to the gift of the Holy Spirit. In a broader sense, in the sense which was current in the Old Testament, the Spirit of God was said to be bestowed upon Jesus to equip him for his Messianic mission 3 34, *cf.* 11 32. S. John is however consistent in his representation that the Spirit, in the special Christian significance, could not be given until Jesus was glorified 7 39, *cf.* 20 22; and he explains Jesus' earlier references to the Spirit, as prophecies of that which was to be given. According to S. Luke also the gift of the Spirit belonged exclusively to the exalted Christ, Luke 24 49 Acts 2 33. It was only then, Acts 1 5, that he justified the testimony of the Baptist, that he should baptise with the Holy Spirit, Mark 1 8.

Corresponding to the importance which was attached to the pouring out of God's Spirit in the prophetic picture of the Messianic age, S. John lays upon it greater stress than does any other Evangelist; and more clearly than any other he shows what constituted the peculiarity of that operation of the Spirit which was the special privilege of the people of the New Covenant. It is as the Paraclete — or Advocate — that the Spirit is most characteristically represented by S. John. The fact that he is a substitute for Christ is pointedly expressed in 14 16, where he is called " another Paraclete," who shall be with the disciples forever, though Jesus separates from them 16 7. In the first instance quoted, it is the Father who sends the Spirit at Christ's prayer: in the second, it is Christ himself who is the sender. As the Spirit is " sent," he is not thought of — as Christ is in I. 2 1 — as an advocate with the Father on behalf of men; neither is he the Advocate or representative of Christ; but, according to the plain sense of the words, he is the representative of God, as Christ himself also was. This therefore is the significance of the Paraclete, that God perpetuates through another representative the close union with his people which they had enjoyed in the presence of Jesus; so that his dwelling in his Church is unending. And this presence of God is so much the closer, because the Paraclete abides not only *with* his people, but is *in* them 14 17. Jesus' departure is therefore their advantage, since it is the condition of their reception of the more, and more universally, effective Paraclete 16 7, who shall guide them into all the truth 16 13, and reveal to them what they were unable to bear from Jesus' lips 16 12. There is even a *beholding* of the Spirit, which is the special privilege of God's people in contrast to the world 14 17.

It is this conception of the Paraclete as the teacher of the truth, which constitutes the most important element in S. John's doctrine of the Spirit, and which brings it into line with his philosophy of salvation. Notwithstanding the mystical note in S. John's doctrine, namely, his conception of the Spirit as dwelling *in* the disciples, he does not represent him as operating upon the will in an irrational manner; but, like Christ himself, through the reason, by the revelation of the truth. As Jesus' saving work is predominantly represented as a revelation of the truth; so likewise is that of his substitute, God's other Advocate. He is "the Spirit of truth" 14 17 15 26 16 13 I. 4 6; or, as it is said in I. 5 6, "the Spirit is the truth." As the Spirit of truth, he is a witness to Christ 15 26, and a guide into all the truth 16 13; and under whatever name he is referred to, he is constantly regarded as a teacher. In 14 26 he is called the Holy Spirit, but his work here likewise is expressed in the same terms: "He shall teach you all things." Even when S. John speaks of the Spirit under the Old Testament symbol of an "unction," the effect of this anointing from the Holy One (namely Christ) is that we "know all things" I. 2 20 27. As it is Jesus' revelation of the truth which is virtually the inception of eternal life; so is it only by a birth from above by water and the Spirit that one can enter into the kingdom of God 3 5. Revelation, spirit and life, are expressly brought into connection with one another in the saying of Jesus: "It is the Spirit that maketh alive; the words that I have spoken unto you are spirit, and are life" 6 63. According to S. John's conception of the Spirit's work,

Christian baptism must be viewed as an "illumination;"—as it was also called in the early Church, after the analogy of the gentile mysteries.

The association of the Spirit with the gift of life, is very subtly intimated in S. John's Gospel under the Old Testament symbolism of *water*. S. John's explanation of one of Christ's sayings as referring to the Spirit who "was not yet," 7 39,—justifies us in seeing this reference in other sayings of the same character. This interpretation of Jesus' words as a prophecy of the Spirit, is connected directly with the saying, "He that believeth on me, as the Scripture hath said, out of his belly shall flow rivers of living water" 7 38. And S. John's interpretation is justified by Is. 44 3, which was probably the Scripture Jesus had in mind, and which expresses the pouring out of the Spirit under the image of a pouring out of water upon a thirsty land. It was however directly from Jesus that thirsty souls were called upon to drink 7 37. Jesus' words were spirit and life, and they were therefore "living water" 4 10, "a well of water springing up unto eternal life" 4 14. This thought has also another association in S. John's Gospel. Jesus' body is the true and eternal Temple 2 19 22, which can indeed be destroyed by the hand of man, but only to be raised again after a short interval by God's power. In this too S. John sees a fulfilment of Scripture 2 22. For what the prophets foretold of the Temple in the coming age, that out of it should proceed a river of blessing and life, Ez. 47 1-12, *cf.* Joel 3 18 Zech. 14 8 Ps. 46 4 Rev. 22 1 *seq.*, is fulfilled of the glorified body of Christ, whence proceed the "rivers of living water" which S. John interprets by reference to the gift of the Spirit. We can probably see in this another reason why he dwells with so much emphasis and with so great mystery upon the flowing of water from Jesus' pierced side 19 34 35, *cf.* I. 5 6-8. That well of living water, which in Jesus had begun to spring 4 14, was not sealed up by his departure from the earth, but chiefly then it flowed like a river from his exalted body.

Although the Paraclete takes the place of Christ and carries out his work, S. John does not intend to represent that the revelation of the Spirit makes a material advance beyond the revelation given by Jesus, or that any other is in the same sense as he the mediator of truth to men. For as in the Epistle the teaching of the " unction " is to the effect that the disciples abide in Christ I. 2 27; so in the Gospel the teaching of the Paraclete is simply a witness to Christ 15 26, a calling to remembrance of his words 14 26, a drawing from his fulness, a taking of his things to declare them unto his disciples 16 14. The Spirit indeed " shall declare things to come " 16 13; but his principal witness is to the past, to the historic fact of Jesus' manifestation, and his witness is in this case co-ordinate with that of the water and the blood I.5 7 8, and with that also of the Apostles themselves 15 26.

Thus Jesus himself remains in an unique sense the mediator of truth and life to believers, and it is thus made possible for those also " who have not seen and have believed " 20 29, to enjoy a teaching from God, and in some sort a vision of Christ.

In the relative independence which S. John ascribes to the Paraclete, we see reflected the high significance of the Spirit as the medium of revelation which the Jewish theology already dimly recognised, and which the Christian theology expressed in the trinitarian formula.

Hitherto throughout this study our attention has been directed almost exclusively to the consideration of *God's* work in the salvation of men: with this paragraph we begin the study of *man's* part in the process of salvation; — namely, his appropriation of the divine gift, and the fruitful consequences thereof. It is not enough that God's work is accomplished; man too has a work to perform. Salvation is primarily the establishment of a relation between God and man, and this demands a mutual work, because it is a relation between person and person. This fact is very obvious, and it was moreover thoroughly recognised by the Jews. Jesus' speeches in the Synoptic Gospels deal predominantly with the conditions of true discipleship, that is with the terms of participation in the kingdom of God. This question is of no less radical importance for S. John: the condition of fellowship with God is expressed by walking in the light, abiding in Christ and in his word. The way however in which this question is answered, constitutes a very marked contrast between the Synoptists and S. John. Jesus' speeches in the Fourth Gospel deal chiefly with the significance of his own person; but this, far from excluding the motive which was predominant in the Synoptical speeches, actually expresses the fundamental condition of salvation — that is of entrance into the kingdom — as the believing recognition of his nature

Believing and Knowing

and worth. In coming to receive the baptism preliminary to entrance into the kingdom, the question was from the Jewish point of view inevitable, "Teacher, what must we do?" Luke 3:10-14. The condition of remaining in covenant relation with God was the keeping of his covenant Law. Consequently Jesus expresses the conditions of eternal life in terms of moral conduct, and with express reference to the Law, Mat. 19:16-21 Mk. 10:17-21. But Jesus' conception of law was so broad, so startling, so hostile to the legalistic spirit of Judaism, as to rouse the suspicion of the scribes. One of them therefore pointedly asks him this question, "Teacher, what shall I do to inherit eternal life?" "tempting him" to entangle himself in a clear contradiction to the Scriptures, Luke 10:25-37. This same question recurs in S. John's Gospel. Jesus interprets Nicodemus' secret visit, and his acknowledgment of him as "a teacher come from God" 3:2, as a request for instruction about the conditions of entrance into the kingdom of God 3:3,5, and he answers it by a demand for moral regeneration, which however is traced back to belief in the Son of man 3:15. This question recurs explicitly in 6:28, "What must we do, that we may work the works of God?" And the ruling conception of the condition of life and salvation is conclusively expressed in Jesus' reply, "This is the work of God, that ye believe on him whom he sent" 6:29. This is S. John's way of disposing of the question which so engrossed S. Paul and S. James (see especially Gal. 3:5 Jas. 2:24). For S. Paul it was an alternative, faith *or* works; for S. James, faith with *or* without works: for S. John the contrast simply did not exist, he had made no such analysis; *faith is the work* which is required for participation in life. With no writer less than S. John however is faith viewed as a work meritorious in itself, and deserving of salvation on account of its moral quality as an act. This striking saying of Jesus does no doubt express the fact that believing is more than a passive receptivity. It is with the labour which is requisite for man's earthly sustenance that he compares the work required " for the meat which abideth unto eternal life ; " but on the other hand this is a meat which is not in any wise to be earned, but " which the Son of man shall *give* unto you " 6 27. Christ's gift to the world is primarily the revelation of the truth ; and this of itself produces in man eternal life and its consequent fruits. But it is not enough that the truth, that is the light, shines *upon* men ; it must be received *into* them. Inasmuch as the truth which Christ reveals is not a bare philosophical conception, but is distinctly within the moral sphere, it can be received only by a moral act — by an act of the will — which is the expression of the deepest disposition of the heart. In this sense, faith is a work, it expresses a positive activity on man's part. And yet, as the condition of salvation, it is regarded with complete abstraction of the intellectual or moral difficulties which have to be overcome, and of the active element of moral choice which it involves: from this point of view the question is simply whether one *has* the truth ; and therefore seeing God and knowing him are, as conditions of life 17 3 I. 3 6, precisely on a par with believing on him. So far therefore is this saying of Jesus from substituting the work of faith for the works recognised by the Law as conditions of life, that it rather does away altogether with the legalistic conception of works. The antithesis between justification by works and justification by faith, which was so radically important in S. Paul's system, and which proved itself so peculiarly liable to misunderstanding, simply does not emerge at all in S. John's theology. This is not merely because the idea of justification is completely strange to his thought; but because he was not even conscious of the rather barren analysis of faith and works, which so puzzled the readers whom S. James addressed. He did not feel the antithesis between salvation by law and by grace. He had not passed through the spiritual crisis which S. Paul experienced in turning from the Law to faith. Therefore, without thinking of the Law as in any sense the antithesis of the Gospel, he expressed the Gospel itself in terms of law; — though practically, as soon as he had come to regard Jesus' revelation of love as the Law, and as the new commandment, the Law in the contemporary Jewish sense was as completely done away as it was for S. Paul. We see in this instance, as in many others, how S. John's theology resolves the apparent contradictions of earlier Apostolic teaching. S. James' discrimination between faith which is accompanied by works, and faith without works, was simply impossible to one who like S. John conceived of faith as imparting the true life, and producing the appropriate moral fruits of life, just in proportion as it was the apprehension of a true knowledge. S. John's theology did not suggest, as S. Paul's did, II. Pet. 3 16, the possibility that moral conduct might in any way be divorced from the idea of salvation, Rom.

§ 6 ¹. His system as a whole was so constituted as to render transparent, beyond the possibility of misconception or of cavil, the relation of faith to salvation: it is simply the willing reception of the light of life. There is a peculiarity of S. John's language which serves materially to prevent ambiguity in his conception of faith: it is that the word faith (πίστις) occurs but once in the writings we are considering; instead of the substantive, he uses the verbal forms, to believe (πιστεύειν), and for the negative, to believe not (οὐ πιστεύειν). This is notable in the first place, because it shows his close attachment to the Aramaic form of expression: he simply translates the Aramaic forms into Greek, though he also makes use of the rich capacity of the Greek tense system. In the second place, and in respect to the point which especially concerns us here, because he thus avoids the ambiguity which was almost inseparable from the use of the substantive. The substantive, faith, may denote either the object of belief, that is, the proposition which is believed, Jude 3; or the absolute act of belief, without reference to any particular object (as commonly in the Epistle to the Hebrews). S. John, by the exclusive use of the verbal form with a distinct reference to the object, lays emphasis neither upon the object, nor upon the act, but upon the fact that the object is appropriated by the subject. It is true that he frequently uses the verb absolutely, as far as the grammatical construction is concerned; but it is never absolute in sense, an object is always clearly implied, and the more obviously because for S. John there is but one object of faith, namely, Jesus. The ambiguity attaching to the word *faith* is exem-

plified in the single case of S. John's use of it I. 5 ₄ ₅:
we are here at a loss to decide whether the faith
which overcometh the world, is the creed, "that
Jesus is the Son of God;" or the act of moral surrender to him. In the next verse however S. John
returns to the verbal form, and disposes of this
apparent alternative by a conception which in a
measure includes both of the ideas which we have
suggested: "And who is he that overcometh the
world, but he that believeth that Jesus is the Son of
God." The orthodox creed is not a victorious power
except as it is received by faith: still less has the act
of faith any moral significance for S. John apart from
its object. Faith in Jesus, if not precisely a virtue,
was highly significant of a man's moral nature; but
faith in itself was not a virtue for S. John, and he
therefore never associates it with any distinctively
moral quality. It is not associated with patience,
nor with hope (ὑπομονή, ἐλπίς), conspicuous as was
the development of these ideas in New Testament
language. With the exception of "hope" in I. 3 ₃,
these words do not occur at all in S. John's writings
(exclusive of the Apocalypse): the *verb* to hope
occurs once 5 ₄₅, in sharp contrast to faith, as the
characteristic of Judaism. It was perhaps because
the word salvation suggested the Jewish attitude of
hope, rather than the Christian attitude of faith, that
S. John avoids its use;— it occurs once 4 ₂₂, "for
salvation is of the Jews." The word Saviour occurs
but twice, and to save (with reference to Jesus' work)
four times. I have consequently been in doubt of
the propriety of using the word salvation as the title
of two of the main topics of S. John's theology, and

I have done so only because it is the term in most current use. Salvation is moreover a negative term, and as such it was unsuited for the expression of S. John's predominantly positive conceptions. He substitutes for it the word, eternal life ; and this which is not only a positive, but a present possession, is therefore not the object of hope but of faith; and faith is more accurately regarded as the appropriation than as the condition of life.

Corresponding to the ruling conception of S. John's theology — the life of God, being manifested, becomes the light of men, and so produces life in them — the idea of faith occupies in his writings a position of the greatest importance. We have only to recall what was said (pp. 130 *seq.*) of the division wrought among men by the manifestation of the light, to understand the crucial importance of the idea of faith in the Fourth Gospel. The ruling motive of S. John's narrative is the representation of the reception which Jesus encountered from the various classes of men with whom he came in contact. S. John, in striking contrast to the Synoptists, represents this in terms of faith: they believed, or they believed not. Unbelief is not a mere negative conception, though even from this point of view its consequence could only be death, because it foregoes the gift of life. But it is more than not knowing God; it is the rejection of him 15 [24]. It therefore not only involved condemnation 16 [8,9], but justified it, in as much as the refusal to come to the light argues an evil life 3 [19,20]. We have already seen that for S. John *the* sin is " that they believe not in me." Believing in him, on the other hand, is the condition of a begetting from God 1 [12,13].

POSITIVE CONCEPT OF SALVATION 179

The foregoing discussion exhibits the place and significance of the idea of faith in S. John's system. It is as simple as it is fundamental; and although S. John employs this conception in manifold relations, although it is a progressive term, corresponding at each stage to the believer's subjective appreciation of the significance of Jesus' Person and the content of his self-witness, progressing also in steadfastness as well as in content; its fundamental significance is nevertheless throughout transparent as the acceptance of Jesus for what he is, and in particular with appreciation of his relation to God. The attitude of men toward Jesus is expressed also in a variety of other ways, though faith has strictly no synonym in the New Testament. Men's attitude toward the light — the figure under which Jesus and his revelation is represented — is expressed by, receiving it or not receiving it 1 5; by coming to it or coming not; by hating it or loving it 3 20 21; and even by believing in it 12 36. We have also the expressions, hearing his voice 18 38 10 3 16 (cf. 8 43 " because ye cannot hear my word"), knowing his voice 10 4 5, coming unto him 5 40 6 35 37 44 45 65, following him 8 12 10 4 5 27 21 19 22, knowing him 10 14 14 17 17 3 (cf. v. 25) I. 2 14 3 1 5 20, seeing him 14 9 I. 3 6, and of course pre-eminently, believing in him.

Jesus as the object of faith is distinguished from all others by a form of expression which is highly significant of S. John's idea of faith as a personal and mystical relation. It is in regard to Jesus alone that men are said to believe in (or unto) him (ϵἰς αὐτόν). It is no contradiction to this that S. John speaks of believing in the light 12 36, for the light is Christ himself. It corresponds to the Aramaic affinities of S. John's language, that he translates the common המין בשום into Greek: πιστεύειν εἰς τὸ ὄνομα. As the Synagogue spoke of faith in God's Name; so S. John speaks of faith in the Name of Jesus I 12 2 23 3 18 I. 5 13. The construction with εἰς makes the Name an object of faith in precisely the same way as Jesus is himself, for the Name is the expression of the person. With reference to God, the construction is not so uniform. Either with the name God, or with such a paraphrase as "him who sent me," the construction is usually the simple dative; but there are two exceptions, in which Jesus speaks of believing *in* God. In both cases the construction is determined by the fact that Jesus would represent the close connection, we might rather say identity, of faith in him and faith in God 12 44 14 1.

Even in relation to Jesus however the simple dative construction is often used; but in these instances we can see that the change of construction denotes a change of sense, and that, instead of the profound New Testament idea of faith and believing, we have here the simple Classical sense of giving credence to one 4 21 5 46 8 45 46 10 37 38 14 11. Belief in Jesus' words and works is expressed by the dative; — though we have in one instance I. 5 10 π. εἰς τὴν μαρτυρίαν. The construction with ὅτι (that) is not uncommon; but it is false to conclude that the object of faith is, therefore, a proposition about Christ, rather than Christ himself; for it is worthy of note that the content of these object clauses — as for example 20 31 "That ye may believe that Jesus is the Christ, the Son of God" — is always a proposition which expresses in the most essential terms what Jesus is, and is therefore equivalent to a definition of what he is as the object of faith; — believing in Jesus as the Christ, the Son of God.

We have finally the expression, to believe through some one or some thing ($\delta\iota\acute{a}$ $\tau\iota\nu o\varsigma$ or $\tau\iota$). The very vision of Jesus as the light ought to be sufficient to elicit faith: but inasmuch as men are able to see only gradually what he is, he does not discard the testimony of external witnesses. It was in the first place *through* the Baptist that men believed in Jesus 1 7; it was then through his works that they learned to believe in him 10 38; through the word of the Samaritan woman 4 39, men were led to a faith which is afterwards confirmed through his own word 14 42; and finally, he looks forward to the time of his departure from the world when men shall believe in him through the word of his disciples 17 20.

Jesus' whole ministry was a schooling of his disciples in faith; they attained but slowly to an adequate appreciation of his nature and dignity. But even an imperfect recognition of him he does not call unbelief, but faith. Every acknowledgment of him which reveals a movement towards the truth Jesus greets as faith. Even the Twelve did not attain to a complete knowledge of the fulness of Christ's Person till after his resurrection: it was Thomas the doubter who first made the adequate confession, "My Lord and my God" 20 28. There was also a strengthening of faith which went hand in hand with its enrichment. Faith is not attainment; it is a stretching out towards it. S. John refuses to consider the possibility that one who had really *seen* and *known* Jesus could fall back again into sin; but no such finality is involved in faith; it might not only exist imperfectly, but cease altogether; — or, as in 8 30-40, turn instantaneously to murderous hate. Not even does the faith of the Apostles continue constant: to their confession of faith just before the Passion, "By this we believe that thou camest forth from God," Jesus answered, "Do ye *now* believe?" — not suggesting a doubt of the reality of their faith, but denoting that the hour approaches when they shall believe no longer 16 30-32. This insecure and changeable faith was indeed far from representing the goal of Jesus' training of the Apostles. It had to attain to a fixed and unalterable confidence; and this too was reached only after the resurrection. To express this faith as an abiding condition, rather than as a momentary act, the ordinary construction with the verb does not suffice; and therefore Jesus uses a substantive expression — "Be not faithless, but *believing* (μὴ ἄπιστος ἀλλὰ πιστός) — for the first and only time on the occasion of Thomas' recovery to Faith 20 27. With faith thus perfected in content and in constancy, the first draft of the Gospel fitly ended.

Closely and emphatically associated with the idea of believing, is that of knowing. The idea of knowing is, corresponding to the whole character of S. John's theology, one of his most important concepts. We dare not ask however what is S. John's idea of *knowledge*; for, as in the case of faith, the substantive is never used. The object of knowledge is not a proposition about God (or Christ), but the person himself. S. John does not speak of knowledge about God, but of knowing him. It is true that knowing, like believing, is often expressed with an object clause (γινώσκειν ὅτι, knowing that); but the propositions which are thus grammatically expressed as the objects of knowledge are in content identical with those which are represented as the objects of faith: "that I am" 8 28, "that thou didst send me" 17 25 "that I am in the Father" 14 20; — as these are believed, so also are they known. The propositions therefore which are thus expressed as the objects of knowledge, are such as define the essential character of the person known, and S. John's highest and most characteristic expression remains that with the direct personal object: to know Christ, to know God 14 7 17 3 I. 2 4 13 14 4 6 7 8 5 20. In S. John's highest use of this term there is distinctly a personal relation involved, an idea of acquaintance. How far he is from thinking of a mere theoretical knowledge, we see in his characteristic employment of εἶδον, which denotes such knowing as comes through seeing; and of θεωρεῖν αὐτόν to behold him 6 40 12 45.

Believing, so far from being contrasted with knowing, seeing, and beholding, is expressly associated with them. The multitude demand of Jesus a sign, in order that they may "see and believe" 6 30; we have in I. 4 16 "we know and have believed," in 6 69 "we have believed and know," in 10 38 the disciples are required to believe in order that they "may know and understand," and in 6 40 we have "he that beholdeth the Son and believeth in him." These ideas are however by no means synonymous, and they are in fact distinctly enough discriminated. Believing is referred pre-eminently to Jesus, whereas the relation of men to God is expressed more commonly as knowing him. The profound breach between the world and God, which expresses itself in their unbelieving treatment of Jesus, is not called unbelief in God, but ignorance of him 7 28 8 55 15 21 16 3 17 25. The result which accrues from knowledge of Jesus is not faith in God, but knowledge of him 8 19 14 7. It corresponds to this, that with reference to the Holy Spirit it is not believing which is spoken of, but knowing and beholding 14 17 I. 4 2 6. Even in relation to Christ, the idea of believing recedes, and that of knowing takes its place, in view of his ascension and the consequent beginning of his more perfect and spiritual relation to his disciples. Whereas in view of his earthly manifestation Jesus demanded, "believe that I am" 8 24; in view of his heavenly it is said, "when ye have lifted up the Son of man, then shall ye *know* that I am" 8 28. In the day when the disciples behold him again, "In that day shall ye know that I am in my Father" 14 20. It is also highly significant of the relation of these two ideas, that while there is great emphasis upon Jesus' knowledge of God 7 29 8 55 10 15 17 25 there is no mention of his faith in God. This is the more remarkable because Jesus represents his own relation to the Father as the perfect pattern, according to which that of his disciples is to be fashioned. As he is in the Father and the Father in him, so are the disciples in him and he in them; as he knows the Father, so do they know him; as he abides in the Father's love, so do they in his; as he keeps the Father's commandment, so do the disciples keep his. But with all these parallels, there is no analogous comparison between his faith in the Father, and his disciples' faith in him. Jesus' relation to God is never expressed in terms of faith. To this we have to add that the truth is represented as the object of knowledge 8 32 I. 2 21 though not of faith;—and so also is love I. 3 16.

Both of these conceptions, knowing and believing, have therefore their own peculiar sphere of application, and the mark which chiefly distinguishes them is this, that believing connotes a characteristic exercise of the will. The fundamental idea of faith, both in Hebrew and in New Testament Greek, is that of trust. This has by no means disappeared from S. John's use of the word. The use of πιστεύειν in 2 24 is indeed unique ("Jesus trusted himself not unto them"); but the idea of trust appears very plainly in the single instance in which we have the expression, to believe *in* God, εἰς τὸν θεόν 14 1. Faith is here contrasted with trouble of heart at Jesus' departure. The construction (with εἰς, " unto ") is here peculiarly significant, when in view of his death, which seems to render him unavailable as an object of faith, he urges his disciples to turn their faith towards God;—not as resting in him, but as struggling towards him. As his disciples had through faith in him been led to a true faith in God; so now he hopes that their trustful faith in God will carry them through this supreme crisis, and preserve their faith in him;—" believe also in me." Faith has in this instance, as in many others, a special relation to difficulties to be overcome. It is for this reason that man's relation to God is expressed rather under the terms of knowledge than of faith. Whatever difficulties a man has to overcome in making a personal surrender of himself to God, they are not such as are represented by the idea of faith. If God is known, he is therewith manifest as man's sole good; and the reasonableness of surrender to him is immediately included in the very idea of God, from which might and majesty are inseparable. But in the case of him whose divine majesty is obscured by his earthly manifestation in the flesh, the act of adhesion is impossible except through an act of trust, and more especially on the part of those who on account of their ignorance of God have many inward hindrances and objections to overcome. It is therefore not without its significance, that the first man whose faith in Jesus is mentioned, is that Nathanael, whose prejudice showed itself in the objection, "Can any good thing come out of Nazareth?" And the Gospel originally ended with the faith of Thomas whose trust in Jesus had been so profoundly shattered that even the testimony of his fellow disciples could not convince him. The victory which overcometh the world I. 5 4, which triumphs over every inward and outward obstacle, and apprehends the Incarnate One as the eternal Word, is an act of trust, and from this the idea of faith gains a significance which differentiates it from that of knowledge.

Eternal Life

"*And the witness is this, that God gave unto us eternal life, and this life is in his Son*" I. 5 11. This verse is one of the most compendious statements of S. John's message of salvation. To understand what eternal life is, and how it is mediated to man and appropriated by him, is to know his Gospel. We have already seen the profound significance of the Father as the source of life, of the Son as the medium of life, and of the children as sharers in the divine life by reason of the divine begetting. We have also seen that life — or at least deliverance from the common doom of death — is directly dependent upon the sacrificial death of Christ. The gift of life, as the positive content of salvation, is more particularly the theme of the chapter upon which we are now engaged, in which we have already considered Jesus' manifestation of the truth which makes eternal life possible for men, and man's believing acceptance of the truth which is the condition of his appropriation of life; which also we shall conclude with the study of the moral fruits of life in the children of God. We have therefore in this section to consider only what eternal life is in itself, and in particular to define it against a common and radical misconception, which represents it exclusively as the product of the revelation of the truth, and its fruition therefore as consisting solely in the contemplative knowledge of God. The purely intellectual and speculative interest which is here presumed in S. John, this barren abstraction of life, would not only place the Apostle in irreconcilable contradiction to all New Testament thought, and set him in close association with Gnostic theories, but would involve an intolerable contradiction in his own thought. Nothing could be more objective and *real* than S. John's conception of life as we have hitherto studied it; imparted as it was out of the fulness of the divine life, and guaranteed for men by Christ's willing surrender of himself to death. We have indeed repeatedly noted those characteristics of S. John's thought — the close association of light and knowledge with life — which seem to justify the opinion which we here reject. Misconception of this phase of S. John's thought is by no means unnatural, but it rests upon a superficial idea of his theology as a whole. It leaves out of account his thoroughly objective conceptions of life, which are however a part of his characteristic development, and can in no wise be explained as mere echoes of current Christian language. More than all, it fails to appreciate the mystical element in S. John's conception of faith and knowledge, as a personal relation, a relation of fellowship with God. Knowledge is at once the condition and the privilege of fellowship with God; and it is in this communion, and not in any speculative knowledge about God, that eternal life consists; — to know the True, and to be in the True, is eternal life I. 5 20. Whatever therefore is a condition of knowledge and fellowship, is likewise a condition of life.

There is no conception which is more commonly noticed as a Johannine peculiarity, and probably none which is really more characteristic, than that of eternal life. The term itself is not peculiar to S. John, he shares it with the Synoptists and with the New Testament writers in general. But his conception of it as a present possession is quite unique and can be paralleled only by partial analogies from other writers. With the Synoptists, eternal life is a prize to be hoped for, something to be "inherited;" the commonest expression is "to enter into life;" or it is said explicitly, "He shall receive in the age to come eternal life" Mk. 10 30. S. John's phrase, on the other hand, is "to have life;" and almost the whole Gospel is proof for the statement that he regards it as a privilege already possessed in the reception of Jesus and the fellowship with God which is made possible through him. It is eternal therefore, not in the sense that it belongs exclusively to the coming age; nor even in the sense that everlasting duration is its dominant note; far less does it represent an indefinite prolongation of man's natural life: it is eternal because it belongs to the eternal sphere of being, which S. John discriminates from the earthly, not according to the category of time, but of place; it is the life which Christ has brought from the heavenly to the earthly sphere. It is an entirely new gift, superadded to man's creaturely and physical life; it is therefore an intensive conception, representing not an infinite prolongation of life, but an unbounded amplification of it; — to have life "more abundantly" or "in excess" 10 10. S. John does not define his idea of life; but strictly speaking he gives no definition of any of his terms. Particularly such ruling conceptions of his theology as light and life, he regards now from one side, and now from another, without seeking by a guarded expression to define them in their totality. In fact the significance of these essentially symbolic terms lies in the fact that they exceed expression, and defy definition. As the figure of light represented to S. John the totality of the divine perfection, so did the figure of life denote the totality of the blessings enjoyed in and through Christ. As surely as this is true, we see the inadequacy of knowledge alone as the definition of life. The most definite proof which is offered in defence of this definition of life, is 17 3 " This is life eternal, that they should know thee the only true God, and him whom thou hast sent, Jesus Christ." But in the first place, this is an example of S. John's way of regarding a conception from but one side at a time; and in the second place, the verse is not a definition even in form; — " This is life, *in order that* they may know." It is quite as apt to represent knowledge as the medium of life, as to define it as its special content. This however is not to deny that the revelation of the truth, and the consequent knowledge of God, is at once the means of imparting life to men, and one of the peculiar privileges of the children of God. This is sufficiently clear from our study of the significance of Jesus' manifestation in general, and in particular from S. John's conception of faith as the apprehension of the revelation of the divine in Jesus. Both knowledge and faith are constantly associated with life, but chiefly as the conditions of life.

There is however another term, which properly comes in between knowledge and life, which it is the more important to notice here because it is so little regarded : it is the term fellowship. Fellowship with God stands in a close, and in a sense in a reciprocal, relation to knowledge. A true knowledge of God is necessary to a true fellowship with him; but fellowship with God cannot but issue in a fuller knowledge. On the other hand it stands in the closest relation to life; like knowledge it is a condition of it, but it is also, and far more adequately than knowledge, the fruition of it. As in

6 56 *seq.* the life which is to be had by participation in Jesus' flesh and blood, is associated with personal communion with him and through him with the Father; so in the Epistle 2 24 25 "If that which ye heard from the beginning abide in you, ye also shall abide in the Son and in the Father: and this is the promise which he promised us, even life eternal" *cf.* I. 5 20. So also in I. 1 3 4, the message of the Gospel is the condition of fellowship with the Church, and that in turn, of fellowship with the Father and the Son; and this constitutes the fulness of joy. Next to eternal life, it is fellowship with God which most commonly serves to describe the peculiar blessedness of the children of God. There is no conception which S. John develops more richly than this; besides the expression, "to have fellowship with him," and the whole range of terms which represent God (the Son, or the Spirit) as "coming," and as "dwelling" among men, we have the formula of mystical union, "being in him" and "dwelling in him." As Christ's mystical union with the Father is the ground and content of his own life 6 57 14 10 19 *seq.*, so must his corresponding communion with his disciples impart to them the same life which he possesses through the Father's abiding in him. It is for this reason that eternal life may be said to be derived from the knowledge of God, because such knowledge is a condition of communion with God. The revelation of the truth in Jesus is therefore life, because it is the way to the Father 14 6.

It is accordant with the whole range of S. John's thought that he thus represents eternal life as a present possession: for he likewise represented all of the blessings of the New Covenant as already realised, at least in germ, with the coming of Christ; — and in this too he is completely in accord with the Synoptical saying, " The kingdom of God is in the midst of you " Lk. 17 21 *cf.* Mat. 12 28. Slight however as is his emphasis upon the developments of the coming age, S. John could not altogether avoid reference to the eschatological bearing of his idea of eternal life. This reference is seen especially in 12 25, " He who hateth his life in this world shall save it unto life eternal." Through this expression, characteristic as it is of S. John, there glimmers the familiar Synoptic contrast between the two worlds. In antithesis to " this world," eternal life here represents the future world. If we are right in this, we may see the same reference in 6 27; " The meat which abideth unto eternal life; " and in 4 14 " A well of water springing up unto eternal life; " and finally in 4 36 " He who reapeth gathereth fruit unto life eternal." In Synoptic language this last would be expressed as a harvesting for the kingdom of God.

This eternal life which is enjoyed in communion with the Father through the Son, which is in fact a participation in the divine life, cannot of course be thought of as subject to decay or death. Therefore in the sixth chapter, quite parallel to the expression, " He that eateth my flesh hath eternal life " 6 54, we have, " If any man eat this bread, he shall live for ever " 6 51 58, and, " that a man may eat thereof, and not die " 6 50. Eternal life has in itself the potency of continuous existence, it is indifferent to death and the dissolution of the body, and is the earnest of an everlasting existence in plenitude of life. Therefore it is said, " He that believeth on me, though he die, yet shall he live" 11:25. But as the resurrection of the body is, in Hebrew and in New Testament thought, essential to the full fruition of life, and as this is not given in the idea of eternal life itself, it is therefore added as an independent conception: " For this is the will of my Father, that every one that beholdeth the Son, and believeth on him, should have eternal life; and I will raise him up at the last day" 6:40 *cf.* 39 54. And whereas in 6:57 the life of the believer is represented as depending upon Christ's possession of life from the Father; in 14:19 the believer's continuance in life is assured by Christ's triumph over death.

The consideration of the consummation of life in the coming age was of the less importance for S. John because he conceived of it as effecting no change which was not in the nature of a mere development of that which the believer already possessed. " He that believeth cometh not into judgment, but hath passed from death unto life" 5:24 *cf.* I. 3:14. We can however understand how from this point of view S. John can speak of life as a present possession, and yet in the expression "the resurrection of life" 5:29 add a completing idea. As he enjoyed eternal life in communion with God, and refers this in turn to knowledge of God, we have the double consequence: that wherever there is faith in Christ as the Son of God, there is eternal life; but that as faith grows riper, and knowledge deeper, the possession and fruition of that life becomes ever fuller and richer. From the knowledge which is by faith, to that which consists in beholding God 17:24 I. 3:2, there is indeed such a progress in the attainment of the perfected life as makes it appear almost a new possession; — though even here we have not to think of a higher life taking the place of a lower, but eternal life is in its very conception the same heavenly blessing, above and below, for ever.

The Children of God — Fellowship

We have already had occasion to note, several times, and from various points of view, S. John's em-
Theology and Ethics phasis upon the idea of fellowship in its double form; — with the Father and the Son, and with the brethren. These two aspects of the Christian fellowship are not separable even in thought: "that they may all be one; even as thou, Father, art in me, and I in thee, that they also may be in us" 17 21. It is one indivisible fellowship; and while on the one hand a man can remain in this community only by abiding in Christ, the vine 15 6; it is on the other hand no less truly a condition of fellowship with God, that the fellowship of believers with one another be realised by observing the commandment of brotherly love I. 3 24. This is justified by the consideration, "He that loveth not his brother whom he hath seen, how can he love God whom he hath not seen?" I. 4 20. The idea of children of God includes two moments of thought: the filial and the brotherly relationship. From S. John's emphasis upon the latter we may see how far he was from regarding eternal life as the mere contemplative knowledge of God. It is a life which is to be exercised in the sphere of the Christian brotherhood, and it finds its satisfaction in the fellowship with the brethren, as

well as in the fellowship with God. The Christian fellowship and eternal life are the two ideas into which S. John has analysed the kingdom of God: as eternal life represents the blessings of the kingdom; so does the brotherhood represent its sphere. Love, the principle of fellowship, directed towards the Father and towards the brethren, is the complete expression of the moral life, the fulfilment of the law of the kingdom. It is at once the privilege and the duty of fellowship. Love is indeed regarded as a commandment; but more characteristically as the spontaneous fruit of the true life. As the Father is love, and as the Son has manifested this love to the world; the life which he thereby imparts to men can be nothing else but a life of love. Likeness of the children to the Father, filial and brotherly affection, is the consequence of their begetting from God, and the natural expression of their condition as children. Love is therefore the test of the presence of true life in man; and in the assurance of meeting this test, lies the filial confidence which casts out all fear.

The above paragraph is a brief rehearsal of the points with which we have to deal in this chapter. It exhibits the relation of the Johannine theology to the Johannine ethics. With no other writer in the New Testament is the relation of theology to life so transparent, so immediate, and so necessary. It is chiefly in the Epistle that the ethical bearing of S. John's doctrine is expressed: S. John's ethics is the blossoming out in the moral sphere of the fundamental ideas of his theology. The strongest proof of the common authorship of the Gospel and Epistle is the fact that the latter is

Likeness to God

the necessary moral consequence of the former. S. John's whole system is in the highest sense practical, and it is capable of being brought to bear with unmatched force upon every individual problem of the moral life. S. John however does not descend to particulars: as in his Gospel he sums up his theology in a few general ideas, so in his Epistle he dwells upon the great central conceptions of morality. The Christian morality is summed up in the idea of likeness to Jesus, which is the same thing as likeness to God, and is expressed particularly by love. S. John does not extol love more highly than S. Paul; it is rather because he includes under this one term the whole catalogue of Christian virtues, that he has received the name, Apostle of love. Notwithstanding his strong emphasis upon the moral walk, he mentions in the Epistle but one concrete case of conduct: " But whoso hath this world's goods, and beholdeth his brother in need, and shutteth up his compassion from him, how doth the love of God abide in him?" I. 3 17. This example serves to display the discrepancy between love which is only in word and in the tongue, and the love in deed and in truth which is ready to lay down life for the brethren, as " he " laid down his life for us I. 3 16 18. This instance recalls the Epistle of S. James 2 15 16, though the single point of comparison rather serves to direct attention to the contrast which between these two epistles is in every other respect so marked. There is in fact no greater contrast within the New Testament than that between the Epistle of S. James, with its many moral precepts unrelated by any moral theory ; and that of S. John, with its single precept of love, as the outcome of his whole theology. The concrete examples of discipline, admonition, and exhortation, with which S. Paul's Epistles abound, stand also in strong contrast to the generalities of S. John's Epistle. This however is referrible in part to the fact that S. John's work is not properly an epistle; it is rather a dissertation accompanying his Gospel, and its aim and destination is too general to allow of reference to the particular situation of any individual community. We learn from the Third Epistle, which is a personal letter, how S. John might deal with particular cases of discipline III. 9 10.

It is however a ground of surprise, that S. John, who was the companion of Jesus throughout his earthly ministry, and who represents Christian morality in terms of likeness to God as he was revealed in Jesus, nevertheless does not — any more than S. Paul — adduce the traits of Jesus' earthly life as the pattern for the disciples' imitation. Here, as throughout the New Testament, it is the imitation of God which is the rule of the Christian life; and it is therefore just those features of Jesus' life in which he most conspicuously transcended the human measure and manifested the divine, which are set forth as the disciples' example. As S. Paul thought of even " the meekness of Christ" II. Cor. 10 1, as manifested transcendently not in his earthly walk, but in his descent from heaven to earth, Phil. 2 3-8 ; so S. John sees love exemplified not in Jesus' kindly intercourse with his disciples, but in his gift of his life for them 15 13, I. 3 16 (his love "unto the end" 13 1), and in God's gift of his Son 3 16 I. 4 9. It is therefore Christ's sacrifice of his life which is the example of love for the world, and when S. John expresses the norm of Christian conduct under any other terms, it is by such general conceptions as, walking in the light, as he is in the light I. 1 7, or, "He that saith he abideth in him ought himself also to walk even as he walked" I. 2 6. The term "walking" represents the most general conception under which conduct can be regarded, and in reference to this last passage, S. Augustine points out that "walking" may be "bearing" only, [*Christus*] *fixus in cruce erat et in ipsa via ambulabat: ipsa est via caritatis.* There is another general conception under which S. John represents the conduct required of the Christian: that is the Old Testament conception of righteousness. As he emphasises the righteousness of the Father 17 25 I. 1 9, and of Christ I. 2 1; so he says, "If ye know that he is righteous, ye know that every one also that doeth righteousness is begotten of him" I. 2 29. Righteousness is with S. John not a soteriological, but an ethical conception; there is no trace of S. Paul's idea of imputed righteousness; on the contrary he warns his readers against the misinterpretation to which this conception was so liable: "Children, let no man lead you astray: he that *doeth* righteousness is righteous, even as he is righteous" I. 3 7 *cf.* v. 10. Finally we have the ritual conceptions of consecration and purity: "And for their sakes I consecrate (or sanctify) myself, that they themselves also may be sanctified in truth" 17 19. And in I. 3 3 "Every one that hath this hope on him purifieth himself, even as he is pure."

As the divine life which was in the Logos became manifested as love, and so was the light of men 1 4;

so must also that eternal life, which has been thereby imparted to believers, manifest itself in them likewise as light and love. This must be displayed not only in such a way as will satisfy themselves of the reality of their possession of life; but that the world may know that they are Christ's disciples 13 35. This is S. John's most characteristic way of representing love in the disciple as the spontaneous fruit of life. It is therefore the more noteworthy that he should express it also in terms of law, as a commandment 13 34. Few as are the ethical precepts attributed to Jesus in the Fourth Gospel, he is nevertheless represented repeatedly as enjoining the keeping of his commandments; and this exhortation is taken up by S. John still more frequently in the Epistle. We have already remarked that S. John has no aversion to the expression of Christian morality in terms of commandment, although his use of the word law ($\nu\acute{o}\mu o\varsigma$) exclusively in reference to Judaism probably indicates his consciousness of the radical difference between the two dispensations. He had however as completely superseded the legalistic standpoint as had S. Paul himself. And his idea of the "new commandment" has nothing in common with that of the "new law" ($\kappa\alpha\iota\nu\grave{o}\varsigma\ \nu\acute{o}\mu o\varsigma$), which early in the second century became current to designate the Christian revelation as the successor and counterpart of the Old Testament Law. It was by including all particular commandments in the one commandment of love according to the measure of God's love, that S. John dissolved the whole conception of Jewish legalism as it was expressed by "the ten thousand precepts of the Torah."

The New Commandment

But if we can find no hint of legalism in S. John's use of the word commandment, we do find in it a proof of his close relation to Old Testament thought, and of his strong emphasis upon the moral walk. S. John had no notion of a contemplative knowledge of God which found in itself its end and satisfaction. To know God was to keep his commandments I. 2 3. Neither did he know of any love of God which was mere feeling, and found its end solely in religious adoration. To love God is to keep his word and his commandments I. 2 5 5 2 *seq.* II. 6. True love is shown in work ($\dot{\epsilon}\nu$ $\ddot{\epsilon}\rho\gamma\varphi$) I. 3 18, as God's love also was displayed in his work 3 16 I. 4 9. Love to Christ shows itself by keeping his commandments 14 21 23, as his love to the Father was shown by fulfilling his commandment 14 31. No one was better aware than S. John that the tree of knowledge is not the tree of life; that it is not knowing, but doing which makes blessed 13 17; that to the having of Jesus' commandments, must be added the doing of them 14 21; to the hearing of his sayings, the keeping of them 12 47. The presence of the light in the world is an admonition to walk in the light 12 35. As God has revealed to men his truth, so is it his commandment that they walk in the truth II. 4.

All commandments are finally included in the one commandment of love to the brethren. S. John actually calls this "the commandment" II. 5, and characterises it absolutely as "his (Jesus') commandment" I. 3 23 4 21, as indeed Jesus himself had called it "my commandment" 15 12 17. In the commandment of love, S. John sums up the whole "message" I. 3 11, and the peculiarity of his ethical conception appears especially in I. 3 ¹⁰ where he represents righteousness as equivalent to brotherly love. This whole conception however is thoroughly in accord with the general characteristics of S. John's thought. As he saw the revelation of God not only in Jesus' words, but in his manifestation as a whole; so, rather than in his individual precepts, it was in the total impression of his life, as love unto the end, that he read the new commandment. As God's revelation of himself was his law for the old covenant, so was the new revelation in Christ the new commandment. It is characteristic of S. John that he represents the imitation of Jesus under the terms of the ethical " ought " (ὀφείλει) I. 2 ⁶ 3 ¹⁶ *cf.* 4 ¹¹.

It doubtless seems strange that Jesus in enjoining love should call it a *new* commandment; as though it had never been recognised in the old Law. It appears indeed as if the Synoptic account also would represent as original with Jesus the summary of the Law in the double commandment of love to God, and to one's neighbour, Mat. 22 ₃₅ *seq.* Mk. 12 ²⁸ *seq.* But on the other hand a certain lawyer summarised the Law in the same terms, Lk. 10 ²⁵ *seq.*; and since these words are a quotation from two of the most familiar passages of the Law, Deut. 6 ₅, Lev. 19 ¹⁸, it would not be strange if they had been a common formula with the scribes. S. John himself meditated upon the paradox involved in the name new commandment. In the Second Epistle he says, "Not as though I wrote to thee a new commandment, but that which we had from the beginning, that we love one another" II. ₅. Again in the First Epistle he calls it, "The message which ye heard from the beginning" 3 ¹¹.

And yet it is also new, at once both old and new, as he says in the second chapter, "Beloved, no new commandment write I unto you, but an old commandment which ye had from the beginning. Again, a new commandment write I unto you" I. 3 7 8 *cf.* I. 3 9 10.

The significance of Jesus' designation of love as a *new* commandment is fully seen only when we study the occasion upon which he first enunciated it 13 31-35. With the departure of the betrayer, Jesus found himself at last alone in the company of his true disciples, whom he had gathered out of the world, and whom he had finally purified. In the constitution of this little company he sees his earthly work finished, and himself and his Father glorified 13 31. As one family they had just partaken of the new covenant meal which Jesus had instituted; he himself looks forward to his departure from them 13 32 33, and to his offering of the covenant sacrifice 17 19. When therefore he gives to his disciples a commandment which shall distinguish them from all the world 13 35, what can this mean but the new law for the New Covenant? This is a commandment which fulfils all that the prophets had foretold of the law of the New Covenant. As a law of love, it is of course written upon the heart, Jer. 31 33 32 40; there is in this law no servitude 15 15, but the only true freedom 8 32 *seq.* God's law in this form ceases to be a burden. As in Mat. 11 30 Jesus says, "My yoke is easy and my burden is light;" so S. John says, "His commandments are not grievous" I. 5 3. Love, as the social law of the New Covenant, is directed specially towards "one another;" as the love of the Father is showed preeminently towards his children, so is their love to be directed especially towards the brethren. This particularism is brought out with great force by the whole character of S. John's representation. It cannot however be considered a retrogression from the standpoint of Mat. 5 44 *seq.;* for in this commandment the whole wealth of Jesus' love comes to expression, and the very constitution of the new community guards it against the narrow and exclusive particularism which marked the national theocracy. In the very announcement of this commandment, Jesus contemplates the relation of his disciples to the whole world 13 35. " Hereby shall all men know that ye are my disciples; " — by a love which in its intensity is displayed especially towards the household of faith; but which triumphs through the Church for the world.

But there is still another respect in which this commandment is new. It is new not only because it was formulated for a new relationship, but because it was enjoined according to a new measure, or measurelessness: " As I have loved you " 13 34. So S. John explains in I. 2 8, it is new, " because the darkness passeth away, and the true light already shineth." The love of Jesus was about to be displayed in its fulness — εἰς τέλος — " Greater love hath no man than this, that a man lay down his life for his friends " 15 13. Henceforth we have a new definition of love; and S. John says, " Hereby know we love, because he laid down his life for us; and we ought to lay down our lives for the brethren " I. 3 16. Here we have a new ideal of love; -- love *in excelsis*. Love with S John is not a mere sentiment of benevolence and good feeling, but a passion; not the correlative of dislike, but of hate and murder; — "not as Cain was of the Evil One and slew his brother" I. 3 12.

It is noteworthy that in S. John's writings there is no commandment of love to God, nor even any exhortation of love to Christ. And yet in the Old Testament this was the commandment which held the first place *cf.* Mat. 22 38. This commandment was there however the more necessary because of the merely formal relation in which the people of the Old Covenant stood to God as Father, and Jesus had actually to remark upon the lack of love to God on the part of the Jews 5 42. But as the relation of the Christian community to God is a real and inward one, founded not only in his election, but in his begetting of them; and on the part of the disciples, in their immediate experience of God, love to God was a matter of course, and throughout S. John's writings it is simply assumed. It is a matter of course that every child of God "loveth him that begat" (τὸν γεννήσαντα), and it is a consequence of this, that he "loveth him also that is begotten of him" I. 5 1. The two commandments are really one: "for he that loveth not his brother whom he hath seen, cannot love God whom he hath not seen;" but as the love of God is the postulate of the Christian community, only the love of the brethren remains to be enjoined as a commandment; — "And this commandment have we from him, that he that loveth God love his brother also" I. 4 20 21. How thoroughly fundamental this idea is with S. John, we see from the turn which it gives to his expression. "Beloved, if God so loved us" — we might expect the obvious deduction, so we ought to love him — but instead we have, "we ought also to love one another" I. 4 11. Likewise in I. 3 16, "Hereby we know love, because he laid down his life for us: and we ought to lay down our lives " — not for him, but — "for one another." This is precisely in accord with Jesus' significant teaching according to the Synoptic Gospels: "Inasmuch as ye did it unto one of these my brethren, even these least, ye did it unto me" Mat. 25 40 *cf.* John 13 20. The only way in which, after Christ's departure *cf.* 12 7 8, the disciples' love can be showed towards him "in deed," is by works of lovingkindness towards his brethren I. 3 17 18.

As S. John comprised in the one idea of love, the whole conception of Christian morality; he must especially have associated with it the ideal of meekness and lowliness of heart, Mat. 11 29, which is so significant a trait of Jesus' precept and example in the Synoptic account. And in fact, just before he enjoined the new commandment he had washed the Apostles' feet 13 12-17. In this symbolic act he represented, more clearly than his words had ever done, the character of the meekness which he required. It was not thinking lowly of oneself, nor adopting a lowly attitude; but assuming a lowly position. It was a yoke, a burden, the willing ("in heart") assumption of the position of a servant; — and this not with reference to God or Christ (a position too obviously just), but towards one's fellow men. "If I then your Lord and Master, have washed your feet, ye also ought" — note the same turn of expression we have been studying — "to wash one another's feet." It was not enough that S. Paul recognised himself "a servant of Jesus Christ," Rom. 1 1; he also says, we recognise "ourselves as *your* servants for Jesus' sake" II. Cor. 4 5.

Corresponding to S. John's representation of the Christian morality in terms of a commandment, he makes prominent also the idea of *reward*. The single passage in which he regards hope as the motive of Christian conduct I. 3 3, implies this conception. There is the same implication in the exhortation to abide in Christ, "that we may have boldness, and not be ashamed before him at his coming" I. 2 28; and in I. 4 17 "boldness in the day of judgment" is regarded as the reward of perfected love. The idea of reward is more expressly represented in the Second Epistle v. 8 than in any other passage in the Scripture: "Look to yourselves, that ye lose not the things which we [or ye] have wrought, but that ye receive a full reward." This is not entirely peculiar to the Epistle. The idea of "wages" is at least figuratively applied to the religious sphere in 4 36. And even Jesus' own work, which is done in fulfilment of the Father's commandment 10 18 12 49, looks for the Father's reward. He expects to be glorified, because he himself had glorified the Father, and had accomplished the work which he had given him to do 17 4 5. And in 15 10 the abiding of the disciples in Jesus' love, is conditioned upon their keeping his commandments; as his abiding in the Father's love, is conditioned upon his keeping the Father's commandments.

We have already discussed S. John's doctrine of the knowledge of God. But S. John employs the word *to know* (both οἴδαμεν and γινώσκομεν) also in another and very different way. The trait we have here to remark belongs exclusively to the Epistle, and is one of its most conspicuous features. It was natural for S. John, who regarded salvation as a present possession, to think of it also as fact which was capable of being experienced and known, of being also tested and verified. Therefore he says: "These things have I written unto you, that ye may know that ye have eternal life" 5 13. And this confidence of salvation is expressed pre-eminently in the last verses of the Epistle: "We know that we are of God, and the whole world lieth in the Evil One. And we know that the Son of God has come, and hath given us an understanding, that we know him that is true, and we are in him that is true, in his Son Jesus Christ." This knowledge of one's salvation is not an intuition, nor does it rest upon any subjective ground: there is no more practical trait in S. John's writings than the character of the tests which he proposes for the assurance of salvation. His fundamental maxim is this: "If we know that he is righteous, we know that every one also that doeth righteousness is begotten of him" I. 2 29. Strongly as the orthodox faith is emphasised as the test for discerning between the spirits of error and the Spirit of truth I. 4 1 *cf.* 2 22 23, it is never expressly mentioned as a ground for a disciple's certainty of possessing eternal life. As love is the test whereby the world may know the disciples of Christ 14 35, and as the false brother is discerned by his lack of compassion towards a brother in need I. 3 17; so has each disciple to judge of the reality of his own salvation by

<small>Confidence</small>

the same objective test, by the proof of a love which is " in deed and in truth " I. 3 18. " Hereby shall we know that we are of the truth " I. 3 19. On the other hand it is said: " Hereby we know that we love the children of God, when we love God and keep his commandments " 5 2. But as love of the brethren is the most objective test, it is that which is most insisted upon: " We know that we have passed from death unto life, because we love the brethren " 3 14. It is practically the same thing when the keeping of his commandment, or his word, is made the test. We have in 2 3 a highly characteristic expression: " Hereby *we know* that *we know* him, if we keep his commandments " *cf.* 2 5. There is also a test of a different character, which is at least not a purely subjective one; that is the witness of the Spirit, who is not only a witness to the historical facts of Christ's life, but a witness also to his abiding presence in his disciples 3 24 4 13. But not only may the disciple be thus confidently assured of that which constitutes the Christian's present possession; in one of the rare instances in which S. John looks forward to the perfection of the believer's life in the other world, he regards that too as the object of knowledge: " We know that when he shall be manifested, we shall be like him, for we shall see him as he is " 3 2. But as the future life is only the perfection of that which we now have, and advances to perfection ever by the same means (that is by the knowledge of God), he might well count that the future life was assured by the verification of eternal life in the present.

Into close connection with the Christian confidence which we have just been considering, S. John brings the idea of prayer: "If our heart condemn us not, we have boldness towards God, and whatsoever we ask we receive of him, because we keep his commandments, and do the things which are pleasing in his sight" I. 3 22. "And this is the boldness we have towards him, that, if we ask anything according to his will, he heareth us: and if we know that he heareth us whatsoever we ask, we know that we have the petitions which we have asked of him" I. 5 14 15.

Prayer

In addition to the great prayer of the seventeenth chapter, there are more frequent references to Jesus' prayers in the Fourth Gospel than in any other. It has been noted that the prayers of Jesus are expressed by the verb ἐρωτάω and those of the disciples, by αἰτέω. The attempt however to explain the principle of S. John's consistent discrimination of these two terms has not been fruitful: they both mean, to ask, and S. John does not use at all the specific word for prayer, προσεύχειν. He comes nearer however to giving a doctrine of prayer than does any other writer in the New Testament. The possibility of address to God in prayer was simply assumed by all Christian writers. Prayer was not a new thing with Christianity; but prayer in the name of Jesus was, and it is upon this S. John dwells.

Participation in the Messianic salvation was in prophecy made dependent upon "calling upon the name of the Lord" Joel 3 5. S. Peter and S. Paul agree in interpreting this as a calling upon Jesus as one who has been exalted to be *Lord*, Acts 2 21 *cf.* 36

Rom. 10 12 *seq.* "Calling upon the name of Jesus" appears together with baptism as the condition of salvation, Acts 22 16. And in Acts 9 14 I. Cor. 1 2 II. Tim. 2 22 Christians are actually distinguished as: "Those who call upon the name of the Lord Jesus Christ." So important was it, and so distinguishing a characteristic of the Christian community, that they addressed their prayers to Jesus as well as to God. This conception appears also in S. John's Gospel, though the early and prevalent misunderstanding of his expression has occasioned even a corruption in the text upon which our Authorised Version is based. We have however even in that text Jesus' express assurance that *he himself* will answer his disciples' prayers: "And whatsoever ye shall ask in my name, that will *I* do" 14 13. But according to the true text (according to the oldest MSS. ℵ B and C and most Versions *cf.* Tischendorf, Westcott and Hort, and Rev. Ver.) prayer is thought of as being offered also directly to Jesus: "If ye shall ask *me* anything in my name, that will I do" 14 14. The omission of "me" in this verse was evidently due to the feeling that there is an incongruity in the thought of addressing Jesus himself *in his name*. From the true text however we see that no such incongruity existed for S. John; we see on the contrary that he does *not* speak of prayer directed to the Father in Jesus' name. In 15 16 the phrase "in my name" is to be connected with "he may give," as appears very clearly in the parallel expression 16 23 (according to the true text. See Rev. Ver.). According to the conception that asking in Jesus' name means direct address to him, we have a suitable interpretation for 16 26: "In that day ye shall ask in my name; and I say not unto you that I will pray the Father for you." Jesus here explains to his disciples that prayers addressed to him do not have to be passed on to the Father. The exalted Christ is so thoroughly the dispenser of all gifts to the Church, that whatever the Father himself gives is given in Jesus' name 14 26 15 16 16 23. This is not in any wise to derogate from the Father's supremacy; for in the verse we have just quoted it is assumed that the Father is pre-eminently the hearer of prayer, and Jesus' power to answer prayers directed to him, is grounded upon the fact that "the Father himself loveth you, because ye have loved me." And in 14 13 the fulfilment of the disciples' petitions by Jesus is said to be a glorification of the Father in the Son. There is a contradiction in Jesus' representation of the possibility of addressing prayers to him: whereas he says in 16 23, "And in that day ye shall ask ($\grave{\epsilon}\rho\omega\tau\acute{\eta}\sigma\epsilon\tau\epsilon$) me nothing. Verily verily I say unto you, If ye shall ask anything of the Father, he will give it you in my name;" we have on the other hand in 16 26 "In that day ye shall ask ($a\grave{\iota}\tau\acute{\eta}\sigma\epsilon\sigma\theta\epsilon$) in my name," and in 14 14 "If ye shall ask me anything in my name, that will I do." It has been noted that the verb used in the first instance is that which is elsewhere used only in reference to Jesus' prayers, and it may be that an understanding of S. John's discrimination between these two words would resolve the contradiction. But a careful study of the passage shows how difficult it is to give them any interpretation which does not involve some confusion. We can see however in a general way, from this whole range of passages that S. John would represent the equivalence of prayers addressed to the Son and to the Father. This was in accordance with the whole trend of his theology. As in the Epistle the reference of the personal pronouns seems often to be to the Father or to the Son indifferently; so even here we have a perfectly neutral expression in regard to prayer: "Ask whatever ye will, and it shall be done unto you" 15 7. In these parting words of Jesus it was in no wise necessary to emphasise the fact that the Father is a hearer and answerer of prayer; but it was decidedly necessary for him to assure his disciples in that moment of farewell that, though they might no longer address him as they had been accustomed to do while he was on earth, nevertheless prayer to the Father constituted intercourse also with *him*, and the Father's gifts were given in *his* name. More than that; they may ask him directly in his name. Hitherto his disciples had talked to him familiarly; but they shall do so no longer 16 23. The old intercourse is about to be broken off, but a new form of intercourse is to take its place, as Jesus ceases to be the object of their social faculty and becomes the satisfaction of their religious nature: "Hitherto ye have asked nothing in my name: ask, and ye shall receive, that your joy may be fulfilled" 16 24. We see especially from this last phrase that in all of his utterances about prayer Jesus aimed at comforting his disciples with the assurance that the intercourse in which they then rejoiced would be continued — though in a new form, *in his name*, that is in such wise as they held intercourse with God — and would be proved by the reception of the gifts which they asked. It is for this reason his words are so unqualified and emphatic:

"Whatsoever ye ask, it shall be done." We have however in the Epistle the qualification, "according to his will" 5 14; and in the verse following we have a thought with which doubtless S. John had often comforted his own heart in view of the apparent failure of his prayers: "And if we know that he heareth us whatsoever we ask, we know that we have the petitions which we have asked of him."

It is after all surprising that S. John's expression "ask in his name" should have been so commonly misunderstood. The phrase more usual in the New Testament is, as we have noted above, "to call on the name of the Lord Jesus Christ." But S. John's expression stands, in one respect at least, much nearer to the Hebrew formula from which they both are derived. The Hebrew קְרָא בְשֵׁם יהוה cf. Joel 3 5 is strictly "to call *in* the name of Jehovah;" and S. John's expression is, apart from his substitution of the word "ask" for "call," the simplest possible adaptation of the Hebrew phrase: "to call (or ask) in the name of Jesus." This interpretation is substantiated unanimously by the Greek commentators. And at all events, from the correct text of 14 14, we see that the understanding of this phrase which at first sight seems to us most obvious — a reference, that is, to the use of the name of Jesus as the concluding formula of prayer addressed to the Father, expressive of the fact that the ground of confident approach is his merit — that this understanding is in reality by no means adequate inasmuch as it fails to afford any endurable interpretation of the expression, "ask *me* in my name." It is a consideration of great importance that we have here an explicit reference by S. John to prayer addressed to Jesus: it is of scarcely less moment that we have this thought expressed by so striking a Hebraism. It is true that the Old Testament furnishes no precise parallel (such *e. g.* as "call upon me in my name Jehovah,") but such an expression would surely not be foreign to the profound Hebraic conception of the "name." Whether or not however we interpret this phrase in the sense of direct address to Christ, we are obliged to recognise in it the pregnant force of the Hebrew idea. And just because in Hebrew the significance of the "name" is so large and so inclusive, we cannot be surprised at the transition (especially in 16 $_{23\,24}$) from "asking in my name" to "receiving in my name," which appears to us so sudden and so harsh. We have in the Old Testament not only "to call in the name of the Lord" (or "in my name") I. Kings 18 $_{24}$ Isa. 41 $_{25}$ 64 $_7$ Zeph. 3 $_9$ Zech. 13 $_9$ (and elsewhere frequently), and, to lift up one's hands in his name, Ps. 63 $_4$; but, to "walk in the name of the Lord" Micah 4 $_5$ Zech. 10 $_{12}$, and various other expressions. For this interpretation in general see Franke, Das alte Testament bei Johannes, pp. 251 *seq.*

It may not be possible to account completely for S. John's use of the word "ask" to the exclusion of the generic word for prayer. But certainly it was not intended to exclude adoration and thanksgiving from the notion of prayer: petition being the most specific conception of prayer carries all else with it. We can see too that the prayer of petition was the most apt to express to the disciples the assurance of continued intercourse with Jesus. For it is only by the answer to prayer that the reality of the mutual relation can be verified. That prayer is not merely the expression of man's attitude towards God, but a veritable means of communication with him, involving also a reciprocal response on his part, is absolutely essential to S. John's conception. For prayer is a part of his doctrine of fellowship. The ground of confidence in prayer, whether it be addressed to the Father or to the Son, is this: " For the Father himself loveth you" 16 27. And the condition of prayer is: " If ye abide in me, and my words abide in you " 15 7. It is therefore as the assurance of continued fellowship with Christ, that the answer to prayer is said to fulfil the Apostles' joy 16 24; — an expression which is almost invariably associated with the fruition of fellowship in one or another of its forms; with one another, or with God in Christ 15 11 16 20 22 I. 1 4. Prayer is not only the fulfilment of the joy of fellowship with the Father and the Son; it has also a relation to the fellowship which exists among the brethren. S. John expressly considers the subject of intercessory prayer: "If any man see his brother sinning a sin not unto death, he shall ask, and he will give him life" I. 5 16. Prayer for a *sinning* brother is a special example of intercession, and it is also its most specific form. The brother who sins is cut off from the Christian fellowship. All sin separates from God; but " there is sin not unto death " I. 5 17; sin that is, which, though it of course cuts one off from life, does not do so irretrievably. As the sinner is thus cut off from the fellowship, and can therefore no longer pray in the covenant Name, it is the duty of the brother to intercede for him, and God will give him life.

When we review from this point the whole of S. John's theology, it is impossible not to recognise it, at once in its profundity, and in its simplicity; in its close attachment to God in Christ, and in its ready application to the moral walk; in its irenic quality, its unity, and its transparency; — it is impossible not to recognise it as the fit legacy of that disciple whom Jesus loved, who for the sake of his witness was kept so long in the world, but now

"Lies as he once lay, breast to breast with God."

www.ingramcontent.com/pod-product-compliance
Lightning Source LLC
Chambersburg PA
CBHW021820230426
43669CB00008B/814